I0820692

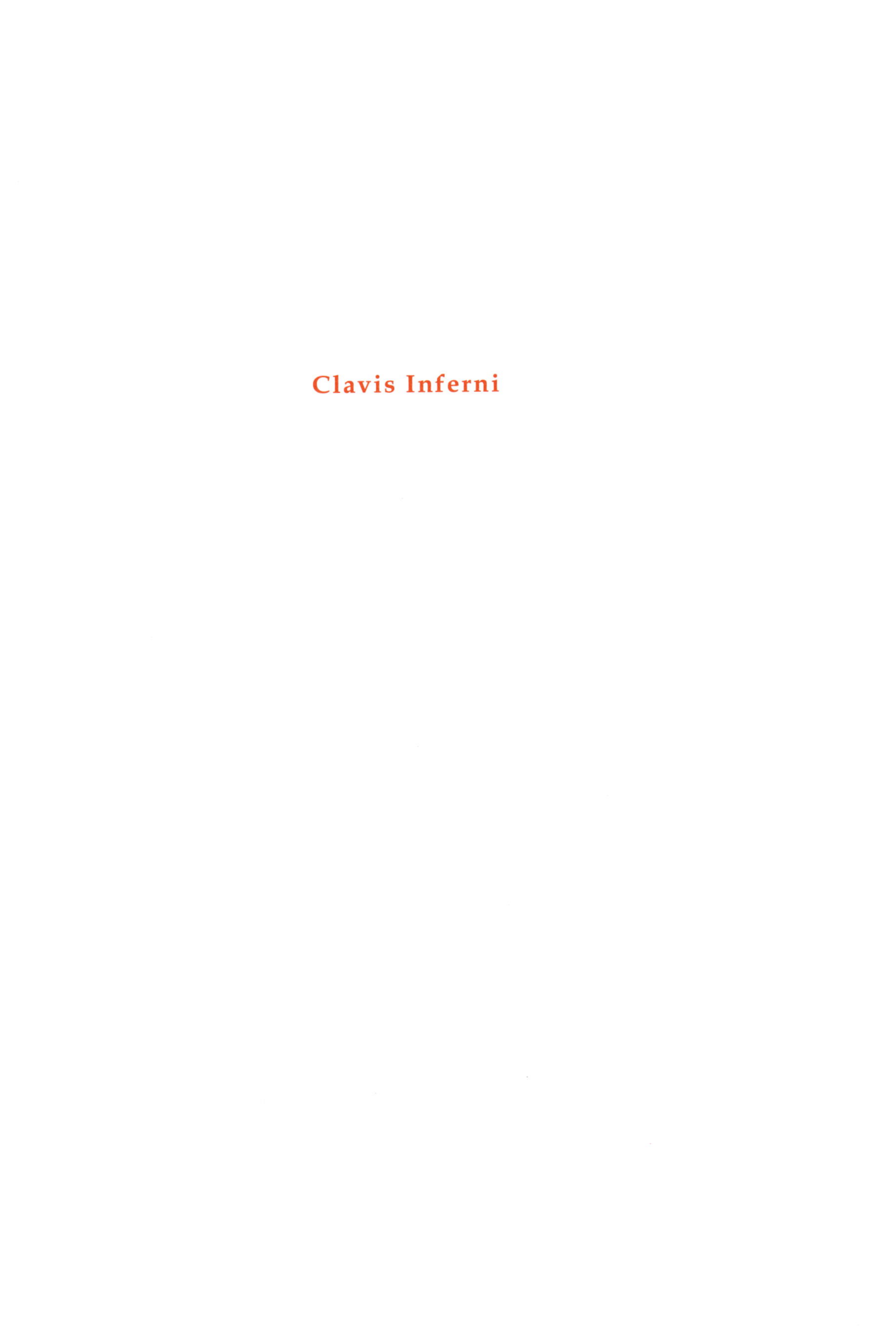

Clavis Inferni

Sourceworks of Ceremonial Magic Series

In the same series:

Volume I – The Practical Angel Magic of John Dee's Enochian Tables - ISBN 978-0-9547639-0-9

Volume II – The Keys to the Gateway of Magic: Summoning the Solomonic Archangels & Demonic Princes – ISBN 978-0-9547639-1-6

Volume III – The Goetia of Dr Rudd: The Angels & Demons of *Liber Malorum Spirituum seu Goetia* – ISBN 978-0-9547639-2-3

Volume IV – The Veritable Key of Solomon– ISBN 978-0-7378-1453-0 (cloth) - ISBN 978-0-9547639-8-5 (limited leather)

Volume V – The Grimoire of Saint Cyprian: *Clavis Inferni* - ISBN 978-0-9557387-1-5 (cloth) – ISBN 978-0-9557387-4-6 (limited leather)

Volume VI – *Sepher Raziel: Liber Salomonis* – ISBN 978-0-9557387-3-9 (cloth) – ISBN 978-0-9557387-5-3 (limited leather)

Volume VII - *Liber Lunæ & Sepher ha-Levanah* - ISBN 978-0-9557387-2-1 (cloth) - ISBN 978-0-9557387-3-8 (limited leather)

Volume VIII - The Magical Treatise of Solomon, or *Hygromanteia* - ISBN 978-0-9568285-0-7 (cloth) - ISBN 978-0-9568285-1-4 (limited leather)

For further details of forthcoming volumes in this series edited from classic magical manuscripts see www.GoldenHoard.com

Other Books by David Rankine

Books on the Western Esoteric Tradition by David Rankine

Avalonia's Book of Chakras (with Sorita d'Este) - Avalonia
Becoming Magick - Mandrake
Book of Gold (with Paul Harry Barron) - Avalonia
Book of Treasure Spirits - Avalonia
Circle of Fire (with Sorita d'Este) - Avalonia
Climbing the Tree of Life - Avalonia
Collection of Magical Secrets (with Stephen Skinner) - Avalonia
Complete Grimoire of Pope Honorius (with Paul Harry Barron) - Avalonia
Cosmic Shekinah (with Sorita d'Este) - Avalonia
Crystals: Healing & Folklore - Avalonia
Fairie Queen (with Sorita d'Este) - Avalonia
Goetia of Dr Rudd: Liber Malorum Spirituum (with Stephen Skinner) – Golden Hoard
Grimoire of Arthur Gauntlet - Avalonia
Grimoire of Saint Cyprian: Clavis Inferni (with Stephen Skinner) – Golden Hoard
Guises of the Morrigan (with Sorita d'Este) - Avalonia
Heka: Ancient Egyptian Magic - Avalonia
Hekate Liminal Rites (with Sorita d'Este) - Avalonia
Horns of Power (with Sorita d'Este) - Avalonia
Isles of the Many Gods (with Sorita d'Este) - Avalonia
Keys to the Gateway of Magic (with Stephen Skinner) – Golden Hoard
Magick Without Peers (with Ariadne Rainbird) - Capall Bann
Practical Angel Magic of Dr. Dee (with Stephen Skinner) – Golden Hoard
Practical Elemental Magick (with Sorita d'Este) - Avalonia
Practical Planetary Magick (with Sorita d'Este) - Avalonia
Practical Qabalah Magic (with Sorita d'Este) - Avalonia
Veritable Key of Solomon (with Stephen Skinner) – Golden Hoard
Visions of the Cailleach (with Sorita d'Este) - Avalonia
Wicca Magickal Beginnings (with Sorita d'Este) - Avalonia

Other Books by Stephen Skinner

Books on the Western Esoteric Tradition by Stephen Skinner

Agrippa's Fourth Book of Occult Philosophy (edited) – Askin, Ibis
Aleister Crowley's Astrology (edited) – Spearman, Ibis
Complete Magician's Tables – Golden Hoard, Llewellyn
Dr John Dee's Spiritual Diaries: the fully revised and corrected edition of 'a True & Faithful Relation of what passed…between Dr John Dee…& some Spirits' – Golden Hoard
Geomancy in Theory & Practice – Golden Hoard, Llewellyn
Goetia of Dr Rudd: Liber Malorum Spirituum (with David Rankine) – Golden Hoard
Grimoire of Saint Cyprian: Clavis Inferni (with David Rankine) – Golden Hoard
Key to the Latin of Dr John Dee's Spiritual Diaries - Golden Hoard, Llewellyn
Keys to the Gateway of Magic (with David Rankine) – Golden Hoard
Magical Diaries of Aleister Crowley (edited) – Spearman, RedWheel Weiser
Michael Psellus 'On the Operation of Daimones' - Golden Hoard
Millennium Prophecies: Apocalypse 2000 - Carlton
Nostradamus (with Francis King) – Carlton
Oracle of Geomancy – Warner Destiny, Prism
Practical Angel Magic of Dr. Dee (with David Rankine) – Golden Hoard
Sacred Geometry – Gaia, Hamlyn
Search for Abraxas (with Nevill Drury) – Spearman, Salamander
Sepher Raziel: Liber Salomonis (with Don[e] Karr) – Golden Hoard
Techniques of Graeco-Egyptian Magic – Golden Hoard, Llewellyn
Techniques of Solomonic Magic – Golden Hoard, Llewellyn
Techniques of High Magic (with Francis King) – Daniels, Inner Traditions, Askin
Terrestrial Astrology: Divination by Geomancy – Routledge
Veritable Key of Solomon (with David Rankine) – Golden Hoard, Llewellyn

Books on Feng Shui by Stephen Skinner

Advanced Flying Star Feng Shui – Golden Hoard
Feng Shui Before & After - Haldane Mason, Tuttle
Feng Shui for Everyday Living aka *Feng Shui for Modern Living* - Cico
Feng Shui History: the Story of Classical Feng Shui in China & the West – Golden Hoard
Feng Shui Style - Periplus
Feng Shui the Traditional Oriental Way - Haldane Mason
Feng Shui: the Living Earth Manual - Tuttle
Flying Star Feng Shui - Tuttle
Guide to the Feng Shui Compass – Golden Hoard
K.I.S.S. Guide to Feng Shui (Keep it Simple Series) – Penguin, DK
Key San He Feng Shui Formulae – Golden Hoard
Living Earth Manual of Feng Shui – RKP, Penguin, Arkana
Mountain Dragon – Golden Hoard
Original Eight Mansion Formula – Golden Hoard
Practical Makeovers Using Feng Shui – Haldane Mason, Tuttle
Water Dragon – Golden Hoard

The Grimoire of Saint Cyprian

Clavis Inferni

sive magia alba et nigra approbata Metratona
the Key of Hell with white and black magic
proven by Metatron

being Wellcome MS 2000

Stephen Skinner & David Rankine

Golden Hoard Press

2023

Published by Golden Hoard Press Pte Ltd
PO Box 1073
Robinson Road PO
Singapore 902123

www.GoldenHoard.com

Acknowledgements

The illustrations from Wellcome MS 2000 have been reproduced with the kind permission of the Wellcome Trust, for which we are duly grateful. Our special thanks go to Bård Sundsfjord for his detailed input on the Black Books of Wittenberg. Joseph Peterson was most helpful in identifying the source of the Cyprian script used on the last page of the manuscript. We should also like to thank Ioannis Marathakis for his help in translating the Greek.

"Yet I am Cyprian, the great magician, who was the friend of the dragon of the abyss. He called me his son, and I called him father. He placed his crown and his diadem on my head. I suckled milk at his right breast. He made my place at his right hand. He subjected to me every power of his. I ascended up to the Pleiades, and they glided by under me like a ship. I learned the whispers of the stars; I took possession of the treasures of the winds. I mastered the whole of astronomy."

- *Spell of Cyprian of Antioch* [1]

"To conclude Dr. Rudd's Doctrine of the Nine Hierarchies of Angels and the better to understand him, that although the glorious Methratton and Raziel may be invocated for some great signal and weighty matters [such as] to prevent ruin of states and kingdoms and persons in great authority, yet it is the opinion of Dr. Dee and Dr. Rudd, and Iamblichus that ancient magician, that it is rarely practiced, since the Olympic powers are sufficient to be invocated and advised with."

- *Keys to the Gateway of Magic* [2]

---

[1] In Meyers and Smith, *Ancient Christian Magic*, PUP, Princeton, New Jersey, 1999, page 154.

[2] This appears in SWCM Volume 2. Metatron and Raziel were seen as weightier than the four classical archangels Michael, Gabriel, Raphael and Uriel. Of these two great angels, the angel Raziel also appears in *Sepher Raziel* SWCM Volume 6 in this same series, and the angel Metatron appears in the present volume *Clavis Inferni* SWCM Volume 5.

Contents

List of Figures

Introduction

This manuscript (Wellcome MS 2000) is attributed to 'M: L: Cypriani', by which is probably meant 'Magistri Ludi Cypriani'. The reference to the 'teacher Cypriani' is almost certainly to Saint Cyprian of Antioch who was reputed to have been a great magician before his conversion to Christianity.

The title of the manuscript, *Clavis Inferni sive magia alba et nigra approbata Metratona,* literally means 'The Key of Hell with white and black magic proven by Metatron'.[1]

Saint Cyprian

We must be careful to distinguish St. Cyprian (Thascius Caecilius Cyprianus) bishop of Carthage from St. Cyprian of Antioch (who was martyred at Nicomedia). It is the latter who had the reputation of a skilled sorcerer before his conversion. But both saints were martyred by the Roman authorities, and both have their feast day in September, which is rather confusing. Saint Cyprian, and his co-martyr and probable mistress Justina, are honoured as saints in the Eastern Orthodox Church with September 26 as the date of their feast, the Catholic Church having removed them both from the roll of Saints in 1968.

The outline of the legend of St Cyprian, which is found in the compilation of Byzantine saints lives by Symeon Metaphrastes, states that Cyprian was a skilled pagan magician of Antioch who had regular and successful dealings with demons. By their aid he sought to seduce Justina, a Christian virgin. She however allegedly foiled a threefold attack by the demons set upon her by Cyprian. Apparently brought to despair by this failure, Cyprian recanted and was converted to Christianity, whereupon he became first a deacon, then a priest, and finally a bishop, while Justina became the head of a convent, or so runs the official story.

During a subsequent persecution of Christians, both Cyprian and Justina were taken to Damascus and tortured. As they refused to recant, they were brought for judgement before Diocletian who had instituted a persecution of both Christians (and Manicheans) from 303 CE till his death in 311 CE, on the rather ambiguous advice of the oracle of Apollo at Didyma. He ordered their execution by beheading on the banks of the river Gallus in Turkey. This story, however, probably only arose later in the fourth century, when it is mentioned both by St. Gregory of Nazianzen and Prudentius.[2]

---

[1] Although it is tempting to translate *approbata* as 'approved' it has a secondary sense, when applied to philosophy or magic, of a theory that has been tested or proven. The word 'proven' (Latin *probatum*) occurs frequently in other magical texts and is applied to recipes and formulae to confirm that these have actually been tested and verified.

[2] See Couliano (1987), pages 215-16, and Ankarloo (2002), Volume 3, pages 216-17.

Saint Cyprian's supposed Confession and description of his training and initiation is quite interesting as a catalogue of the magical centres of the day, even if it was not actually penned by the Saint himself.[1]

> "I am that Cyprianus, who, vowed to Apollo from his infancy, was early initiated into all the arts of the dragon. Even before the age of seven I had already been introduced into the temple of Mithra: three years later, my parents taking me to Athens to be received as citizen, I was permitted likewise to penetrate the mysteries of Ceres lamenting her daughter, and I also became the guardian of the Dragon in the Temple of Pallas.
>
> Ascending after that to the summit of Mount Olympus, the Seat of the Gods, as it is called, there too I was initiated into the sense, and the *real* meaning of their [the Gods'] speeches and their clamorous manifestations (*strepituum*). It is there that I was made to see in imagination (*phantasia*) those trees and all those herbs that operate such prodigies with the help of demons; ... and I saw their dances, their warfares, their snares, illusions and promiscuities. I heard their singing. I saw finally, for forty consecutive days, the phalanx of the Gods and Goddesses, sending from Olympus, as though they were Kings, spirits to represent them on earth and act in their name among all the nations.
>
> At that time I lived entirely on fruit, eaten only after sunset, the virtues of which were explained to me by the seven priests of the sacrifices.
>
> When I was fifteen, my parents desired that I should be made acquainted, not only with all the natural laws in connection with the generation and corruption of bodies on earth, in the air and in the seas, but also with all the other forces grafted (*insitus*) on these by the Prince of the World in order to counteract their primal and divine constitution. At twenty, I went to Memphis, where, penetrating into the Sanctuaries, I was taught to discern all that pertains to the communications of demons [*Daimônes* or Spirits] with terrestrial matters, their aversion for certain places, their sympathy and attraction for others, their expulsion from certain places, certain objects and laws, their persistence in preferring darkness and their resistance to light. There I learned the number of the fallen Princes, and that which takes place in human souls and bodies they enter into communication with.
>
> I learnt the analogy that exists between earthquakes and rains, between the motion of the earth and the motion of the seas; I saw the spirits of the Giants plunged in subterranean darkness and seemingly supporting the earth like a man carrying a burden on his shoulders.
>
> When thirty, I travelled to Chaldaea to study there the true power of the air, placed by some in the fire and by the more learned in light. I was taught to see that the planets were in their variety as dissimilar as the plants on earth, and

[1] This version is translated, and modified, by H P Blavatsky from the French of the Marquis de Mirville, who purportedly translated it from a Latin manuscript found in the Vatican. The comments in square brackets are by Blavatsky. It may of course just be a romantic fiction, but nevertheless an instructive one. See also *Secreta Cyprian* in Bodleian, Digby MS 30.

> the stars were like armies ranged in battle order. I knew the Chaldaean division of Ether into 365 parts, and I perceived that every one of the demons who divide it among themselves was endowed with that material force that permitted him to execute the orders of the Prince and guide all the movements therein. They [the Chaldeans] explained to me how those Princes had become participants in the Council of Darkness, ever in opposition to the Council of Light.
>
> I got acquainted with the Mediatores, and upon seeing the covenants they were mutually bound by, I was struck with wonder upon learning the nature of their oaths and observances.
>
> Believe me, I saw the Devil; believe me I have embraced him when I was yet quite young, and he saluted me by the title of the new Jambres,[1] declaring me worthy of my ministry [initiation]. He promised me continual help during life and a principality after death.[2] Having become in great honour [an Adept] under his tuition, he placed under my orders a phalanx of demons, and when I bid him good-bye, "Courage, good success, excellent Cyprian," he exclaimed, rising up from his seat to see me to the door, plunging thereby those present into a profound admiration."[3]

Cyprian left his Chaldean initiator to set up as a sorcerer in Antioch where he became an accomplished magician "surrounded by a host of disciples... distributing love-philtres and dealing in deadly charms 'to rid young wives of old husbands', and to ruin Christian virgins." The latter activity brought him into conflict with the local Christian community. According to them he was finally converted, baptised, and "laid at the feet of Anthimes, Bishop of Antioch, all his books on Magic, finally becoming a martyr and saint." Of course the story goes that one of his books escaped the flames and became the *Cyprianus*. It is highly unlikely that any such book survived, but this story was meant to authenticate the efficacy of the magic of the *Cyprianus*. Because of his reputation, a number of books of magic began to circulate purporting to be from his pen. We must therefore first examine two versions of the Cyprianus not directly connected with the present manuscript.

The Iberian Book of Saint Cyprian

A Latin version of the book of St. Cyprian entitled *Cyprien Mago ante Conversionem* is claimed for 1460, but is more likely to have been published in the nineteenth century. The *Libro de San Cipriano* (*The Book of St Ciprian*) started circulating in Spain in the same century and *O Antigo Livro de São Cipriano* (*The Ancient Book of Saint Cyprian*), which is full of prayers and spells, sold widely in the

---

[1] Jannes and Jambres were two famous Egyptian magicians referred to in 2 *Timothy* iii. 8 as the Egyptian magicians who withstood Moses in front of Pharaoh. These magicians were not only mentioned in the Bible, but were known to Classical writers such as Pliny and Apuleius.

[2] Principality is a high angelic rank.

[3] The phrase "seeing him to the door" suggests that Cyprian was at the court of a senior Chaldean magician, rather than in the presence of the arch-fiend himself.

Portuguese speaking world, especially in South America.

Although these books refer to Saint Cyprian, they appeared centuries after his death and could not possibly have been written by him. In fact the first known printed edition of the *Libro de San Cipriano* came out in 1849. According to the title page it was:

> "the Book of Saint Cyprian, taken from a manuscript. Made by the Saint himself, who teaches how to undo all the spells made by the Moors in this Kingdom of Portugal, and also how to find the places where riches can be found."

Why St Cyprian, who lived in Antioch in Turkey should be interested in Portuguese Moorish spells is not explained. The book was taken from Portugal to Brazil and became widely used in popular sorcery allied with the practice of Umbanda and Candomblé. A number of editions of the work appear under titles such as *The Great and True Book of St. Cyprian, The Only Complete Book of St. Cyprian, The Authentic Book of St. Cyprian,* and so on. All these explain that Saint Cyprian, the sorcerer of Antioch, is not the same as the famous bishop of Carthage.

There are two versions of the *Libro de San Cipriano*. The first was simply a Spanish version of the *Gran Grimoirio* (*Grand Grimoire*) falsely attributed to Cyprian to help it sell. The second format was less concerned with evocation and more with protection from demons, prayers, exorcisms and instructions on how to cure disease. Other sections included a list of the 174 treasures of Galicia[1] which can be released by the application of the right magical formulae; the Prayer of the Guardian Angel; the 50 'mysteries of witchcraft' from the time of the Moors; medical spells; the treasures of magic (including a way to capture rather than evoke a devil); a black magic procedure used to destroy a marriage; the prayer of the Black Goat; the use of a skull lit with a candle; an explanation of the hidden powers of hatred and love; and the powers of magnetism. All this is interlaced with pious prayers of popular Catholic religiosity. It appears to have been solely an Iberian production. The present manuscript is not related to this book except in name only.

The Scandinavian Black Books of Wittenberg

Meanwhile in the more northerly parts of Europe yet another tradition grew up around Saint Cyprian. He is the reputed author of a number of seventeenth and eighteenth century manuscript grimoires that circulated in Scandinavia, especially Norway. These grimoires were often referred to as 'Black Books' (*svartebøka*), and the German town of Wittenberg was often quoted as the source of this knowledge. The background of these books is deftly summed up by Bård Sundsfjord:

---

[1] Mention of Galicia and Asturias (where it was called the *Ciprianillo*) are clues to its probable origin in Northern Spain.

"The information on the Black School is nearly all in the Scandinavian languages as far as I know and comes from folk stories and the black books themselves. The only exception to this is the book edited by Mary Rustad, *The Black Books of Elverum.* [1]

In Scandinavia it is Cyprianus who is the 'great wizard' as opposed to Germany where Faustus is the main character, and has many black books penned in his name. The other Grimoire famous in Scandinavia is the *Sixth & Seventh Books of Moses.*[2] There are also stories of offshoots from the Black School in various Scandinavian countries, one in Stavanger in Norway, in Stockholm, Sweden, in Denmark etc. These are of course only legends, but at least one may actually have some base in reality. The school in question was in Sweden in Eastern Goeringe in a forest called Bjoerkhult, where a man took students and taught them magic. The story goes that he had an 'original Cyprianus', and the students learned the arts that he had the most interest in and penned his own book (something that was of utmost importance), before travelling home to his own community he came from, to practise his arts. This was sometime during the late 1700s.

According to one early nineteenth century source, the Cyprianus was a "horrifying, nefarious tome known by everyone in the countryside as 'Cyprianus', whereby one can conjure up and put down the devil and get him to do just as one commands, and whose pages teach how to recover lost goods, cure all kinds of disease, remove curses, find buried treasure, turn back the attacks of snakes and dogs, and more..."

The local Wizard or 'black book man', as he was often referred to, was a man that people both had the utmost respect for, and also feared. He was called if a witch had set a curse on someone, if people were sick, if there were hauntings in a house or elsewhere, and he always had a cure, a spell or practical advice. In times of few doctors and priests, one can understand the importance of such people. Not all the Wizards were good, though. There where those who used the black book for evil ends; to control people and have their way with the town's women! These Wizards were not that well liked.

The wizards were credited with being able to control the Devil and his demons and to having them working for him. But there was another class of wizards also, a class that people had little respect for, but much fear. These were often poor people, roaming the countryside, and the only chance of some 'respect' they had was to pretend to be a Wizard, or to actually be one.

Many of the more vicious Wizards were believed to have a pact with the

---

[1] Two such manuscripts, found in 1994, are printed in facsimile with an English translation in Rustad (2006). Strangely the first of these claims to have been written by Bishop 'Johanes Fell' [or Sell] from Oxford in the year 1682. This was in fact Johannes Fell (1625-1686) Dean of Christ Church and Bishop of Oxford who published an edition of the works of St Cyprian (of Carthage not of Antioch) in 1682. It is therefore probably a mistaken attribution, rather than a translation into Norwegian of an English Black Book written by the Bishop of Oxford.

[2] Joseph Peterson, *Sixth and Seventh Books of Moses*, Ibis, Berwick, 2008.

Devil, but only two of the known Black Books from Norway contain any such instructions for acquiring pacts with Lucifer.

Many of our priests were credited with having the black book, these priests had 'studied in Wittenberg'[1], and they became known as 'black book priests'. One such priest is the famous Norwegian priest and poet/writer Peter Dass.

The journey the student took to Wittenberg for a Wizard to learn the arts, and get the Cyprianus, might be seen as an initiatory journey. Many of the Wizards were reputed to have been on journeys lasting for a year or two, and when they returned they bought back the Black Book with them. The book often stayed in the family, and it was not unusual for the son to take over the 'post' from his father as a Wizard.

The introductions in the black books often referred to the Black School of Wittenberg, like this one: "The *Art Book of Cyprianus* was first discovered at the academy of Wittenberg in the year 1722 and after printing was distributed in several places and kingdoms, where it was hunted down and burned, finally it was again found at the Castle of Copenhagen in a marble stone coffin, written in parchment" or the "*Cyprianus Art Book* written in the academy at Wittenberg Anno 1354 and subsequently found at Copenhagen Castle Anno 1665 in a marble stone coffin written on parchment." In other versions the Marble stone coffin is at the academy of Wittenberg itself, and the date is 1509.

There are about 150-200 known existing exemplars of Black Books in Norway today. On a rare occasion a new one pops up, like the two translated by Mary Rustad. I would very much like to recommend this book to you, as it is the only other known source for the Cyprianus in English that I am aware of.

The contents of these books vary, but many are coloured by the rural period in which they were written. Much of the contents concern the well being of man and beast, hunting, amulets and the kind, and only a small part actually concerns conjurations/evocations of demons. The books can often be classified by the owner's interests and livelihood, and can be seen as 'fisher/hunter books' (containing a great deal of charms spells and amulets for these purposes), 'military books' containing amulets for protection in war, having the strength of seven men, arts for getting spirits to get money, obtaining sex with women, etc.

Some of the immigrants who went from Scandinavia to the USA took with them the Black Book traditions from their own countries. This is an interesting part of history. I do remember seeing a book at one time in English on Amazon, I think, about a priest who 'knew more than the Lords prayer' (which was a way of saying that the person was in possession of magical secrets).

In parts of the US today, namely in Pennsylvania, there are people of Dutch

---

[1] Wittenberg on the Elbe River was famous for being the home town of Martin Luther, and hence was the birthplace of Protestant reform in 1517, as well as of Black Book sorcery. It did not officially become a town till 1293, it was a cultural centre in the 15th century, and the University of Wittenberg was founded in 1502. The Zaubererakademie was reputedly the School of sorcery. Johann Faust was also reputed to have lived in Wittenberg.

heritage who still practises the same arts that can be found in the Black Books of Scandinavia. They call themselves Hexenmeisters, and function in pretty much the same way that the old Wizards of Scandinavia did. The strictly religious Mennonites [founded 1530s] and old order Amish [founded 1690s], and other people still seek these Hexenmeisters out when there are problems to solve. Particularly health problems, since the woman of these religious communities often refuse to take their clothes off for doctors.

The books these Hexenmeisters mainly use are the *Long Lost Friend* by Georg Hohmann (which contains much of the Black Book material from Scandinavia which was imported from Germany) and the *Sixth & Seventh Books of Moses*. A good book on this subject is: *Hex and Spellwork: The Magical Practices of the Pennsylvania Dutch*, by Karl Herr. A good movie with this theme, based on real events, was also made called *Apprentice for Murder* and starring the actor Donald Sutherland as a Hexenmeister.

My own interest in the black books, and in the 'original Cyprianus' has been there since childhood. My grandfather "knew more than the Lords Prayer." He could staunch blood, remove pain, remove warts, etc. People that knew this contacted him and were helped. He learned from his father, who also practised these arts, and from my grandfather I learned the arts and inherited the documents containing the 'family secret.' [1]

Of the 150-200 examples of Scandinavian Black Books that are extant, no two have exactly the same content, each being modified by the magician who copied it. One such magician or cunning man was the Dane, Anders Ulfkjaer.

However the present manuscript is not part of the tradition of Scandinavian Black Books. Just as the contents of this present manuscript do not match the printed Spanish or Portuguese *Cyprianus*, so they do not match the currently published Cyprianus 'Black Books' of Wittenburg.

The Heptameron

In fact the present unique manuscript is definitely part of the Solomonic tradition of grimoires, although it may not look like it at first glance. It draws many of its invocations from Peter de Abano's *Heptameron*.[2] These are often found in other magical manuscripts of the 16th to 18th century which are firmly part of the Solomonic tradition. A classic example of invocations from the *Heptameron* appearing in other magical texts has been documented in our edition of the *Lemegeton* (*Goetia*).[3] Even some versions of the *Key of Solomon*[4] contain material drawn from de Abano's *Heptameron*. Let us look at some of the other features of this manuscript.

---

[1] From a private communication with the present author.

[2] See Agrippa, *Fourth Book of Occult Philosophy*, Ibis Press, Berwick, 2005. Parallel passages found in the *Heptameron* are footnoted throughout the transcribed text section.

[3] Skinner & Rankine, *The Goetia of Dr Rudd*, Golden Hoard Press, Singapore, 2007, pages 193-211.

[4] Skinner & Rankine, *The Veritable Key of Solomon*, Golden Hoard Press, Singapore, 2008.

Metatron

The central presence of Metatron in this work is unusual, as he is not as frequently found in the grimoires as other archangels like the classic quartet of Michael, Gabriel, Raphael and Uriel. This is not to say that he is ignored, as he does turn up in the *Key of Solomon* (Mathers), the *Grimorium Verum*, and the *Nine Celestial Keys.*[1] Where Metatron is particularly evident is the Merkavah tradition of Kabbalah, particularly in the Book of *3 Enoch*. Here he acts as guide to Rabbi Ishmael and protector of the Rabbi from the fury of the other angels in the seventh Hall.

Metatron is described as the Prince of the Divine Countenance (*Malach ha-Panim*) or Angel of the Divine Countenance (*Sar ha-Panim*). As the first Sephirah on the Tree of Life, Kether, represents the Divine Countenance, so its archangel Metatron is the representative of the Divine Countenance. This is seen in the *Shiur Qoma,*[2] where it says, "This is the seat of Metatron, the Lord of the Presence which is written with one-letter [i.e. Aleph, whose numeration is one]." The same text even goes so far as to identify Metatron with Adam Kadmon, the archetypal divine man made in the image of God.

In the context of the present work, one of the most significant qualities of Metatron is that all the keys (i.e. divine secrets) are committed to him.[3] Thus it is entirely appropriate that he should be in charge of the key of hell (or *clavis inferni*).

The letters of Metatron add to 314, which is also the numeration of *Shaddai*, a title of Yesod and Divine Name, showing the role of that Sephirah as described in the *Thirty-Two Paths of Wisdom*, to "dispose the unity … without diminution or division". This association is emphasised in *Sepher Raziel*, as is Metatron's human origin (as the transformed patriarch Enoch son of Jared):

> "Metatron is all the actions and power of Shaddai, of all the one power. It is proclaimed, Metatron comes from below, pure and clean."[4]

The meaning of the name Metatron is unclear, as like his brother Sandalphon, it is not a Hebrew name. Amongst the speculations, it has been suggested that the name is derived from the Greek Meta-Thronos, "He who serves behind the Throne", referring to his high position in the presence of God.[5]

Metatron is a paradox, described as being one of the oldest of the Archangels who is also known by the name of 'Youth' (*Na'ar*). He is described in *3 Enoch*

---

[1] See *The Keys to the Gateway of Magic*, Skinner & Rankine, 2005.
[2] *Sh'ir Qoma* 'Measure of the Divine Body' from the *Sefer Raziel HaGadol*.
[3] See *Zohar* i.37b, i.55b, i.181b, i.223b, iii.171b.
[4] Steve Savedow, *Sepher Rezial Hemelach*, Book 3, Part 4, page 196.
[5] Lieberman, 'Metatron' in Gruenwald, *Apocalyptic and Merkavah Mysticism*, pages 235-241.

as having seventy names, and several lists give Yahoel as the first of these. As with the name of the Lesser Jao,[1] it contains the divine name within it.

The Kabbalistic scholar Gershom Scholem gives evidence to suggest that Metatron was originally the secret name of Michael,[2] and that this tradition survived until the fourth century CE. The connection to Michael, whose name is used in the constraining triangle of the *Goetia*,[3] hints at his role as the supreme angel for the constraint of demons, as does the Shemhamphorash reference in *3 Enoch* 9, where Enoch-Metatron says:

> "I was enlarged and increased in size till I matched the world in length and breath. He made to grow on me 72 wings, 36 on one side and 36 on the other, and each single wing covered the entire world..."

The description of the transformation of Enoch into Metatron emphasises his fiery nature, common to the highest of the angels, rather than the air that some of them are conventionally made from. This fiery nature is emphasised in the picture of Metatron in the present text *Clavis Inferni*.

> "Forthwith my flesh was changed into flames, my sinews into flaming fire, my bones into coals of burning juniper, the light of my eye-lids into splendour of lightnings, my eye-balls into fire-brands, the hair of my head into hot flames, all my limbs into wings of burning fire and the whole of my body into glowing fire."[4]

Metatron is the archangel referred to in *Exodus* 23:21 "Take heed of him, and hearken unto his voice; be not rebellious against him; for he will not pardon your transgression; for My name is in him." In this context again we see the commanding and constraining power associated with Metatron, above all the other angels. He is also referred to in *Exodus* 33:14 when God says "My Countenance will go with you, but I will depart", and in *Isaiah* 63:9 as "the angel of his presence".

In the Blessings Scroll of the Qumran literature the term "angel of the Countenance" is also used for the High Priest, and the identification of the magician with Metatron to command the demon princes, when Metatron himself exemplifies the man transformed into an angel, may follow the same principle.

> "May you be as an Angel of the Countenance in the Abode of Holiness, and may the glory of God be upon you and His magnificence all around. May you attend upon the service in the Temple of the Kingdom and cast a lot with the Angels of the Countenance and the Congregation of the *yahad* with Holy Ones, for everlasting ages and time without end."[5]

---

[1] This is clearly a form of IAO as a derivative of IHVH, indicating his power as the first archangel of God.

[2] Gershom Scholem, *Major Trends in Jewish Mysticism*, 1995, page 68.

[3] See for example Sloane MS 3648.

[4] *3 Enoch*, 15.

[5] Qumran texts 1Q28b: IV:25-26.

The Four Demon Kings

Another remarkable part of the present manuscript is its inclusion of the four Demon Kings which are illustrated in a rather quaint fashion both as Kings and in their bestial form.[1] In each illustration, each King is given his own seal, which as far as we can tell is unique to this manuscript.

Another very interesting feature of the illustrations of the four Demon Kings is that each is accompanied by the name of the angel and godname that constrains him. This name is written in a magical script called 'Crossing the River'. The Demon Kings, Archangels and divine names [2] are paired as follows:

Maymon	Gabriel	ALHINV [ALHIM] [3]
Egyn	Uriel (Haniel)	AChTh
Urieus/Orieus	Michael	IHVH
Paymon	Raphael	SHDI (Shaddai)

There is much confusion about which direction each King governs, and various authorities give different arrangements. The direction is of seminal importance, as it conditions the direction the operator should face whilst invoking.[4]

Maymon, which is usually taken as a variant of Amaymon by the addition of the initial 'A', first occurs in the *Heptameron,* the text which is probably the most important single influence on this present grimoire. In the *Heptameron* Maymon is the King of the Angels of the Air ruling on Saturday. The name Maymon does occur as the King of the East in the Grimoire of Pope Honorius (1670), but this position is occupied by Urieus in the *Clavis*.

The variant name (or mis-transcription) Uricus is somewhat more obscure, occurring in *Magia Mathematica* (1589-90) by Giordano Bruno as King of the East.

If we look at an early manuscript of Abramelin (1610), it has Oriens, Paimon, Ariton and Amaimon as four of the eight sub-princes, gathered together in a manner which clearly indicates their connection as a group, as is also seen in the conjurations where the single largest group of spirits belonging to these four collectively (111 out of 316 spirits). The correlation between Demon

[1] Skinner & Rankine, *Keys to the Gateway,* Golden Hoard Press, Singapore, 2005, page 229.

[2] IHVH and SHDI are common divine names, but AChTh ('the one') is less familiar, and probably should have been AChD ('unity' as shown in Figure 7).

[3] This is correct Hebrew and 'Elohenu' means 'our God'. It can be found transliterated this way in Reuchlin, *De Verbo Mirifico*, page 38. It is possible that אלהים ALHIM was intended, but the original scribe copied מ M as נו NV, thereby changing ALHIM into ALHINV, later shortened to HINV.

[4] See Tyson's edition of Agrippa, *Three Books of Occult Philosophy,* Llewellyn, St Paul, 2005, Book 2, Scale of Number 4: Oriens, Paymon, Egyn, Amaymon, and page 533. See also Stephen Skinner, *Complete Magician's Tables,* Llewellyn, St Paul, 2006, Tables M62-M64.

King, his direction, Element and animal form in the *Clavis* is shown in the table on the next page.

King	**Urieus/Orieus**	**Maymon**	**Paymon**	**Egyn**
Direction	East	South	West	North
Element	Fire	Air	Water	Earth
Animal	Ouroboros	Bird	Sphinx	Bear

Other texts from the same period show variations in the arrangement of the cardinal directions of these four Demon Kings which has varied considerably over the centuries. The *Clavis Inferni* attributions agree with Agrippa and the *6th & 7th Books of Moses.*

Manuscript	Date	East	South	West	North
Agrippa, *De Occulta Philosophia*	1531	Oriens	Amaymon	Paymon	Egyn
Key of Solomon Additional 36674	Mid-late C16th	Eggye	Amaymon	Paymon	Egyn
Pseudomonarchia Daemonum	1563	Amaymon	Ziminiar	Corson	Goap
Scott, R, *Discoverie of Witchcraft*	1583	Amaymon	Ziminiar	Corson	Goap
Abramelin	1610	Oriens	Amaimon	Paimon	Ariton
Lemegeton	1641	Amaymon	Ziminiar	Corson	Goap
Grimoire of Pope Honorius	1670	Maimon	Amaymon	Paymon	Egin
6th & 7th Books of Moses	1734	Oriens	Amayon	Paymon	Egyn
Clavis Inferni	1757?	Urieus/ Orieus	Maymon	Paymon	Egyn

The animals depicted in the images of the Demon Kings are extraordinary. The red winged and crowned ouroboros is associated with, and encircles, Urieus. It is similar to the illustration in Faust's *Magia Naturalis et Innaturalis* (Figure 2).

From the fifteenth century dragons were often represented as winged serpents, like that seen in the present image, especially in alchemical texts. Many different attributions may be made to the dragon, but the most obvious from an alchemical viewpoint, is its cyclic and transformatory nature. The fiery red colour of the dragon, standing out from the black of the other creatures, suggests that the elemental attribution is of Fire in the East.

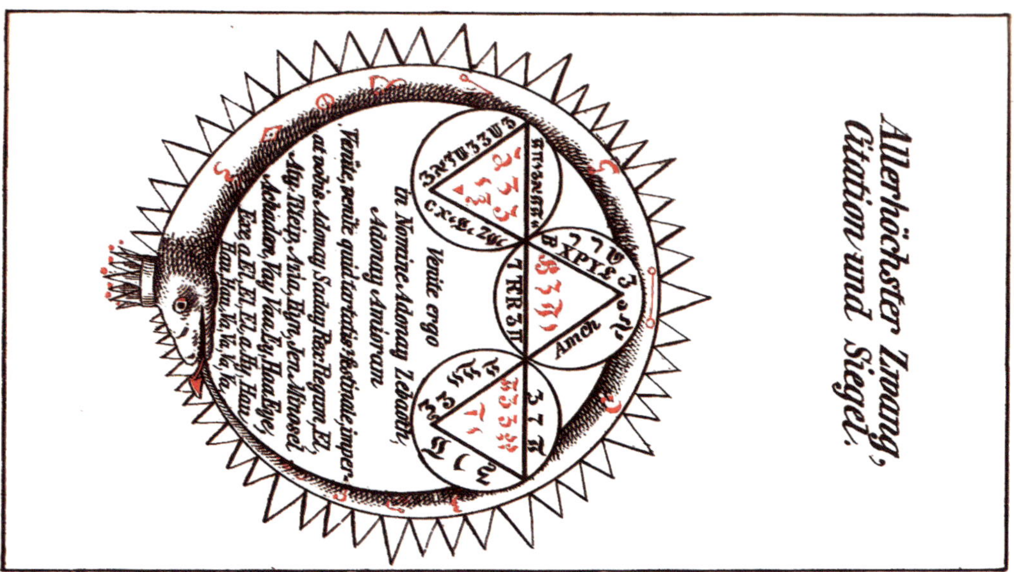

Figure 1: Crowned Ouroboros from Faust's *Magia Naturalis et Innaturalis*. Note the invocation is the same as that used in the *Clavis* [1] and ultimately derived from the *Heptameron*. The Magical Script however is not the same as that used in *Clavis*.

Figure 2: Mephistophiles in bestial form from Faust's *Magia Naturalis et Innaturalis*. Compare this with Egyn the Demon King in Figure 9.

[1] See pages 54 and 68 of the present text.

The bird, symbolising Air is attributable to the South. The animal depicted with Paymon resembles a black-horned sphinx or manticore. The last animal, the Earthy bear-like creature with Egyn, is almost identical to the image of Mephistophiles[1] in Faust's *Magia Naturalis et Innaturalis* (1849) which has obviously been contributory to the present text.

In fact not only does the Faust book have similarities of illustration, but it also has a magical script which is very similar to the one found on the last page of *Clavis Inferni*. The obvious conclusion is that the author of the *Clavis* was influenced by the Faustbooks as well as by the *Heptameron*. The existence of a manuscript entitled 'Julius Ciprianus den XII & D[r] J[ohannes] Faustus Dreyfaices Höllen Schwang [Dreifacher Höllenzwang]' in the Copenhagen Royal Library testifies to this connection. Another manuscript showing the cross-fertilisation of the Faustbooks and the Cyprianus is 'Cyprian's Invocation of Angels, with his Conjuration for the Spirits guarding Hidden Treasures' published as a Faustbook grimoire in volume 2 of Scheible's *Das Kloster*. Both these manuscripts specialise in treasure hunting magic.

Dating the Manuscript

The date on the title page appears to be written as 'MCCCCCCLLXVII', but this is not a correctly expressed Roman numeral, as 'LL' never usually occur together in Roman dates. Assuming this date still has meaning, we can interpret it in a number of possible ways. If 'LL' is interpreted as 2 x 50 = 100 then the date might be interpreted as 1717.

If you look at the last letters carefully you can see that the fourth character from the end was originally an 'L' which has been later over-written with an 'X'. As both the handwriting and the Wellcome's catalogue suggest a date in the late seventeenth century, we could surmise that the original date was meant to be MCCCCCCLLLVII or 1757, but that somebody decided to set the date back by 40 years to give it a more aged provenance. In any case none of these dates are correctly written Roman numerals, and the most likely dates 1717 or 1757 should have been written as MDCCXVII or MDCCLVII.

Another piece of the puzzle which might have some bearing on this manuscript dating is a German theologian called Johann Cyprianus (1642-1723). He was famous for his interest in things esoteric, and was a collector of rare books on alchemy. In fact perhaps the most beautiful alchemical text, the *Splendor Solis,* was owned by him, and inscribed with his name. His niece Mrs Priemer sold the manuscript to Edward Harley, who later sold it to the British Museum, where it remains in the British Library as Harley MS 3469. If the present Cyprianus manuscript was by him, then a 1717 date is more likely.

---

[1] From the first Faustbook till 1755, he was spelled 'Mephostophiles. In *Magia* the first 'o' was replaced with an 'i', and the last syllable fluctuates between -philes, –phiel, -philus and -phiels.

Cryptography

In the *Oldtidens Sortebog fra Aaret 1400 funden ved Udgravningen i en Ruin af en gammel Borg* ('The Ancient Black Book from the year 1400 found during the excavation of an old castle ruin') published in 1892 in Chicago there is a reference to a 'key'. The key consisted of a piece of paper folded into the back cover, which simply stated that the Latin formulae should be read in reverse. This is very interesting, as not only is it signed 'Cyprianus'[1] but the key to many passages in the present manuscript is to read the Latin in reverse. The most commonly used cryptographic trick in the *Clavis* is the reversal of some Latin phrases in the middle of a normal Latin sentence. We have shown these reversals in the text in the first instance on the upper left hand page as they appear in the manuscript, but printed in red to indicate their reversal. Then below we have set them with the Latin reading in the correct direction, but retained the red type to facilitate comparison with the original passage.

Likewise many words in Greek and and Hebrew are first printed in that language on the upper left hand page, then transliterated in the Expanded text at the bottom of the same left hand page. Some Greek letters are used to convey whole words, like Α and Ω stands for 'Alpha and Omega', the 'Beginning and the End', a title of God. The Greek letters ΜΡΓΥ or MRGU stand for the four Archangels, Michael, Raphael, Gabriel and Uriel. Σ or 'S' (or sometimes Ω or 'ω') stands for *spiritus*, or spirit. In other cases, such as the bottom of the title page, the transliteration of Greek letters reveals Latin words, in order to further hide the meaning.

Likewise, there are a series of characters which are variations on the letter 'V' and inverted 'V' which stand for Latin words like *vivi, vici* and *veri*.

In addition the manuscript uses three different magical scripts. Some passages are written in the magical script called 'Crossing the River' and these have been transliterated in each case in the transcription of the text, at the bottom of the left hand page.[2] In the illustration of The Holy Spirit the angel names are captioned in yet another magical script called 'Malachim script'.[3]

There is also a third set of characters (primarily used on the last page of the manuscript), which are called the 'Cyprian' alphabet which are in fact derived

---

[1] Strangely, in the introduction to this book, purportedly written by a monk, 'Cyprianus' is described as a beautiful 14th century Mexican nun who suffers torture and incarceration at the hands of a priest! Other weird and wonderful distortions of the identity of Cyprianus include an evil Dane kicked out of Hell for being too wicked (in Holsten, Denmark), a legendary 10th century German monk Jonas Sufurino who was given the book after conjuring up the Devil on a mountaintop one night (Brooken, Germany) and a tender and decent student (Norway).

[2] See Stephen Skinner, *The Complete Magician's Tables*, Golden Hoard Press, London & Singapore, and Llewellyn, St Paul, 2006, Table L48.

[3] Ibid, *The Complete Magician's Tables*, Table L49.

from the *Polygraphia* of Trithemius,[1] and maybe also from Schwente's *Steganologia*. These also occur in Harley MS 3420, a 1614 version of the *Magical Calendar*.[2]

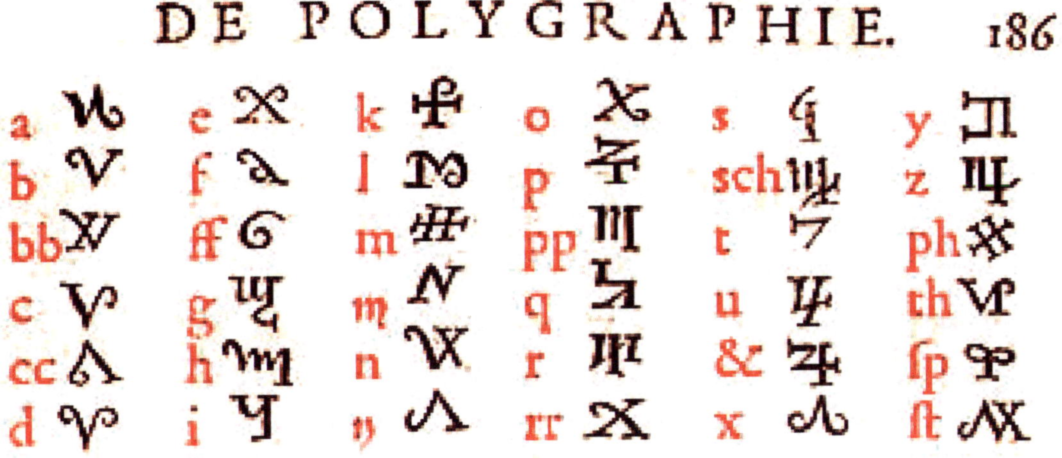

Figure 3: Cyprian characters from Trithemius's *Polygraphia*.

These Cyprian characters are similar to some of the characters used in the Faustbooks, which as we have seen also contributed several illustrational motifs.[3] Finally there are a group of as yet unidentified characters primarily used only on the last page of the manuscript (see pages 32 and 60). Some of these also occur in the sigils of the seven planets in the *Magical Calendar*, but probably have deeper roots in the grimoire tradition. For example □ and X are attributed to Jupiter, and Λ and ҁ to Mars, while the seal of Haniel ℜ is similar to a sigil attributed to Mercury. However none of that makes much sense.

Provenance

The manuscript was purchased by the Wellcome at Sotheby's sale on 29th March 1912. Its provenance before that is not clear, although there are some indications from internal evidence that it might have been owned or even written by Robert Curzon, 14th Baron Zouche (1810-1873) a traveller and collector of early Biblical manuscripts, who was fascinated by cryptography, monastic manuscripts and magic. If this is the case then the manuscript creation date of 1857 seems possible. In an earlier book in this series we

[1] J.Tritheme, *Polygraphie*, 1561, page 186. They are also referred to there as the 'characters of Cicero'. See Figure 3.

[2] See Appendix II.

[3] The term 'Cyprian script' refers to the ancient script of Cyprus, but this is not the script used here. Cyprus used that script to communicate with neighbouring countries like Crete, Egypt, and Phoenicia. This was often referred to as 'Cyprian Script', and it derives from the Minoan script. In the Cairo Museum there are tablets from the 15th and 14th century BCE, which were discovered at Tel el Amarna in Egypt, containing the text of a letter from the King of Alasia, Cyprus, to the Pharaoh and referring to the exchange of Cyprus copper for Egyptian silver, written in that script.

demonstrated that Curzon owned at least one of the manuscripts of the *Key of Solomon* and signed his name at the back of it in a magical cipher similar to that used in this present manuscript.[1] Curzon also known to have collected in his travels several Syriac manuscripts which contained the story of St. Cyprian and his conversion. So he would have been well able to put together the present manuscript. However this is just a tentative suggestion.

The Manuscript

The manuscript is written on vellum, and preserved in a brown velvet binding over wooden boards, with gilt stamped leather covers secured with a brass clasp. The manuscript only has 21 pages, which are not numbered. We have taken the liberty of moving the two illustrations orphaned at the end of the text so they are grouped with the manuscript's other illustrations. Accordingly the pagination is 1...9, 20, 21 followed by the text pages 10...18. Page 19 is blank.

When we discovered the manuscript in 2004, we could not locate any references to its contents or its vivid images despite extensive research. As far as we know the manuscript is totally unique, and although there are many Cyprianus manuscripts, there does not appear to be another cast in this mould. Work on other projects pushed our publication plans back, but we continued to work on deciphering the mixture of linear and reversed Latin, Greek, and magical scripts.

We subsequently used one of the images on the cover of *The Keys to the Gateway of Magic* (Sourceworks of Ceremonial Magic, Volume 2) in 2005. Since we made details of *Clavis Inferni* public, this grimoire has been consistently gaining more and more interest from researchers and practitioners alike, even to the point where one writer used exactly the same image from this manuscript that we had used, on the cover of his book, without extrapolating on its origin or explaining its significance.

---

[1] Skinner & Rankine, *The Veritable Key of Solomon*, Golden Hoard Press, London & Singapore, and Llewellyn, 2008, page 68.

Key to the Symbols

The symbols have been decoded by reference to the illustrations in the manuscript and also by using the three types of magical script. Malachim script and the famous 'Crossing the River' script are both found in Appendix I and both appear in Agrippa.[1] They are ultimately derived from Hebrew and were used as a form of secret writing for Hebrew magical texts. They are quite different from the so called 'Theban' script which was based upon the English alphabet not the Hebrew one. The third script, the Cyprian alphabet, from Trithemius's *Polygraphia* appears in Appendix II.

Archangels	*Zodiac*
= Gabriel	= Aries
= Greek Γ (*gamma*) = Gabriel	= Taurus
= Michael	= Gemini
= Greek M (*mu*) = Michael	= Cancer
or = Tzaphkiel [?]	= Leo
or = Tzadkiel	= Virgo
= Raphael	= Libra
= Raphael	= Scorpio
= Greek P (*rho*) = Raphael	= Sagittarius
= Kamael	= Capricorn
= Haniel	= Aquarius
= Greek Υ (*upsilon*) = Uriel	= Pisces

[1] Agrippa, *Three Books of Occult Philosophy,* Book III, Chapter XXX.

Alchemic/Letter	*Elements*
= R	= = Terra = Earth
= T (as in Tartar)	= Ignis = Fire (see Alpha)
= S (as in Sulphur)	= = Aqua = Water
	= Aer = Air
Latin Contractions	
= Veri = true	= Benedictus = Blessing
= Aeternum = Eternal / Ever	= Benedictissimus
= Vivi = [of the] Living	= Theos = Deus/Dei = God
= Vovis [?] = vow to God	= Domini = Lord
= Veri = [of the] true	= Mundi Sanctus? = holy world
= omnipotens = Almighty	= Sanctus = Holy
= orationem = prayer	= Coelos = Heavens
= Volvere = Revolving?	= Aeternum = Eternal
= Christ	= tripartitus = Threefold
= Princeps = Chief	= 'con-' (before) or '-us' (after)
= Hora = Hour	= Sanctus Spiritum = Holy Spirit
= M Paraclete?	= Pater = Father

= the Sign of the Cross	= Nomine = Name
= que	= per
= quam (as in 'sisquam')	
Greek	
= alpha & omega	= Alpha & Omega
Planets	
= Venus	= Mercury
= Jupiter	= = = Sol = Sun
= Luna = Moon	= Saturn
= Mars	= Star
Cyprian script used in the Clavis	
= = A	= N
= B	= N
= C	= Ph
	= PP
= E	= R
= I, J	

	= O?
Title Page Author Name Characters	
Sundry & Uncertain	
	= Ninth Heaven?
	= clavis = key
	= inferni = hell?

Clavis Inferni

Wellcome MS 2000

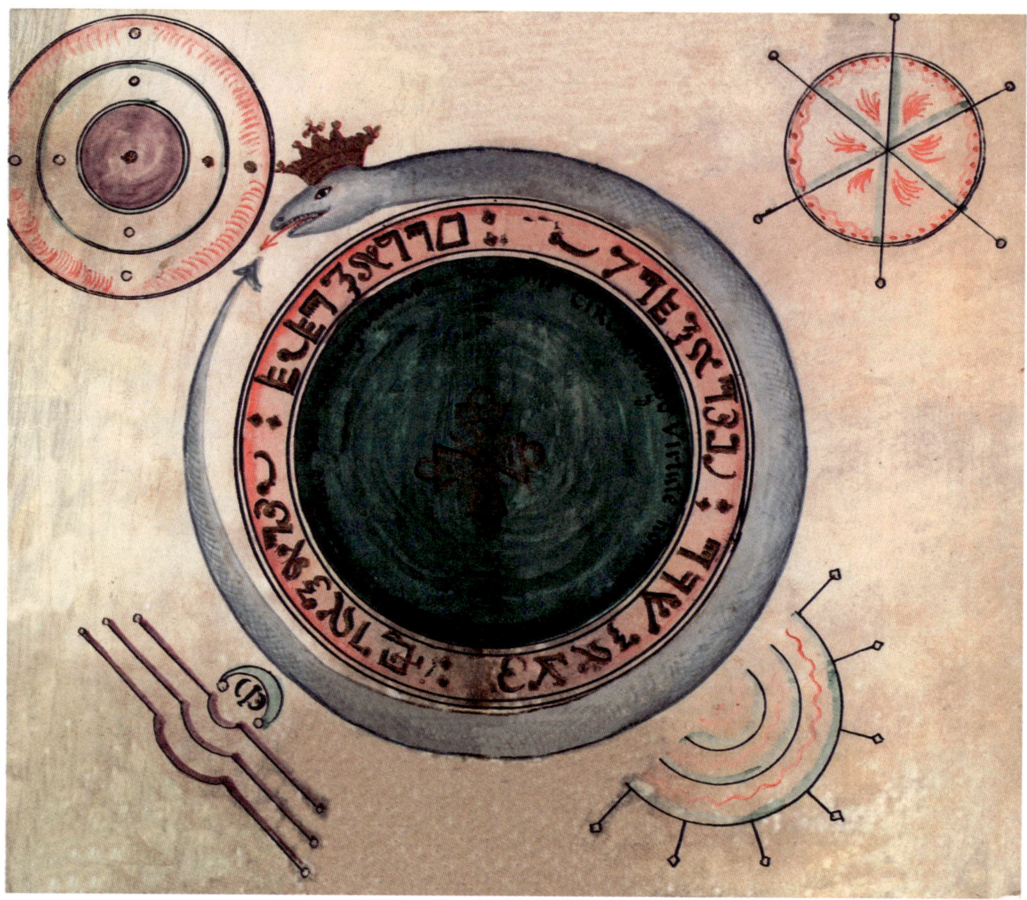

Figure 4: The Serpent Ouroboros and the seals of the Four Demon Kings.

The crowned serpent Ouroboros encircles a green disc around which is written: "Ego me circumcingo Virtute horum Nominum. Qiubus [*sic*] hic Circulus est consignatus" which means "I surround myself with the virtue of these names with which this circle is sealed." This indicates the importance of the direction in magical workings. The Seals of the four Demon Kings are located at the four corners outside the serpent. The text, written in 'Crossing the River' script, is the same that appears on the pages showing the Four Demon Kings, and shows the godnames and Archangelic names that control the Demon Kings:

Egyn	Uriel (Haniel)	AChTh	North[1]
Maymon	Gabriel	HINV [ALHIM]	South
Urieus/Orieus	Michael	IHVH	East
Paymon	Raphael	SHDI (Shaddai)	West

The centre contains a stylised Maltese Cross.

[1]

---

[1] This page is a fold out. North is located in the direction of the Ouroboros head.

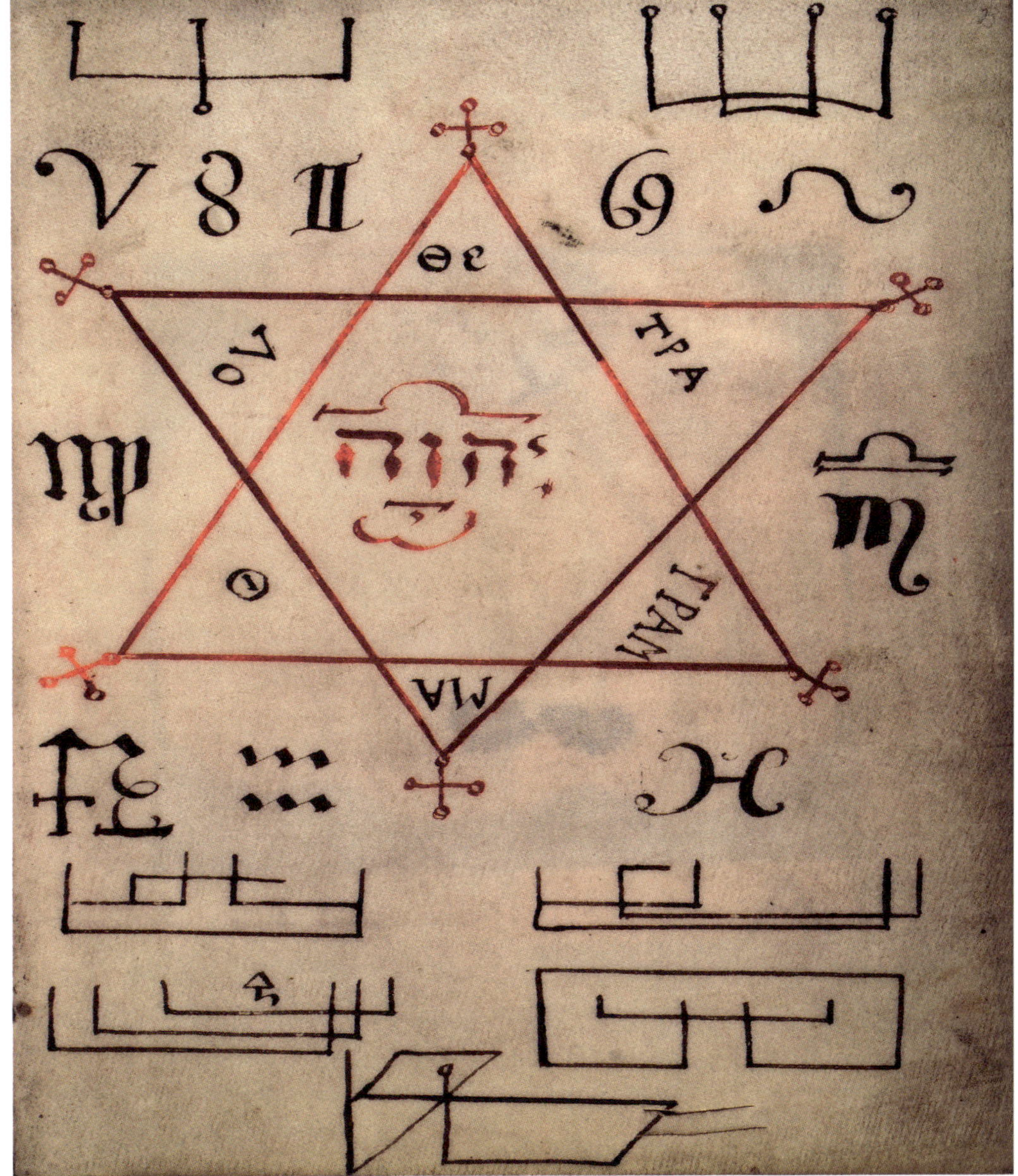

Figure 5: The Hexagram.

In the centre is IHVH between Heaven and Earth, with an extra Yod fecundating the Earth. Clockwise from top, the vertices of the hexagram contain Θϵ-Τρα-Γραμ-Μα-Θ-ον (Te-Tra-Gram-Ma-T-on). Surrounding the hexagram, from top left are the 12 Signs of the Zodiac in three rows: Aries, Taurus, Gemini, Cancer, Leo; Virgo, Libra, Scorpio; Sagittarius, Capricorn, Aquarius, Pisces. Above are the Seals of Och and Phul, and below Aratron, Bethor, Phaleg, Hagith, and Ophiel which are the 7 Olympic Spirits of the 7 planets.

[2]

Figure 6: The Holy Spirit.
[3]

The Holy Spirit

The picture shows the Holy Spirit, with flames coming from his eyes, and a two-edged Sword emanating from his mouth, walking on the clouds. Present are the seven candles of the *menorah* and the seven stars, both Jewish symbols which also appear in *Liber Lunae*. Exactly the same symbolism is seen in the etching by Albrecht Dürer (1471-1528) of 'St John Beholding the Seven Candlesticks', shown in Figure 12. These images come from *Revelation* 1:12-20 illustrating the fact that this illustration is part of standard Christian iconography.

Although the central figure is referred to in *Revelation* 1:13 as "like unto the Son of man", it is more likely to be the third member of the Trinity, the Holy Spirit. In *Revelation* 2:7 the figure is just referred to as "the Spirit". Revealingly in *Revelation* 1:18 the figure says "I am he that liveth...and have the keys of hell and death" which is obviously why this image is so important to the *Clavis Inferni.* Furthermore, *Revelations* 1:20 explains that the seven stars represent the seven angels of the seven churches, and by extension the seven planetary angels whose names are inscribed around the picure in magical script.

The triangle above the picture features the extended Tetragrammaton written in the form of the Pythagorean Tetraktys, in Celestial Character script I - IH - IHV - IHVH, and numerically adding to 72 (the Shemhamphorash). On either side of the triangle are two smaller triangles containing one and three yods (י) representing god as the Monad and the Trinity. In the top corners is the Hebrew for the four Archangels, MIKAL (Michael), RPAL (Raphael), GBRIAL (Gabriel) and URIAL (Uriel) plus AT (את Aleph to Tau which is the Hebrew equivalent of A to Ω, the first and the last letters of the Hebrew and Greek alphabets respectively) and AP (alpha rho).

On either side of the picture are a more complete set of the seven planetary Archangels written in Malachim script (see Appendix I), and beneath each Archangel's name is its Seal as used later in this manuscript. On the left: RPAL (Raphael), KMAL (Kamael), TzDQIAL (Tzadkiel). On the right: GBRIAL (Gabriel), MIKAL (Michael), and HANIAL (Haniel, often equated with Uriel). Below the picture is a Z-shaped symbol that could represent Tzaphkiel (whose name appears above it in magical script).[1]

Immediately below the illustration is AΩ (the first and last letters of the Greek alphabet in black). The A and Ω are symbols commonly used as a Divine Name, and are specifically mentioned in *Revelations* 1:11. Underneath these letters are two symbols for Eternal God. At the bottom in the centre is a symbol made of three vertical bars cutting a horizontal line, sometimes used to represent Jesus Christ.

---

[1] Rather confusingly, this same symbol appears to represent Jehovah at the bottom of folio [10] on page 52.

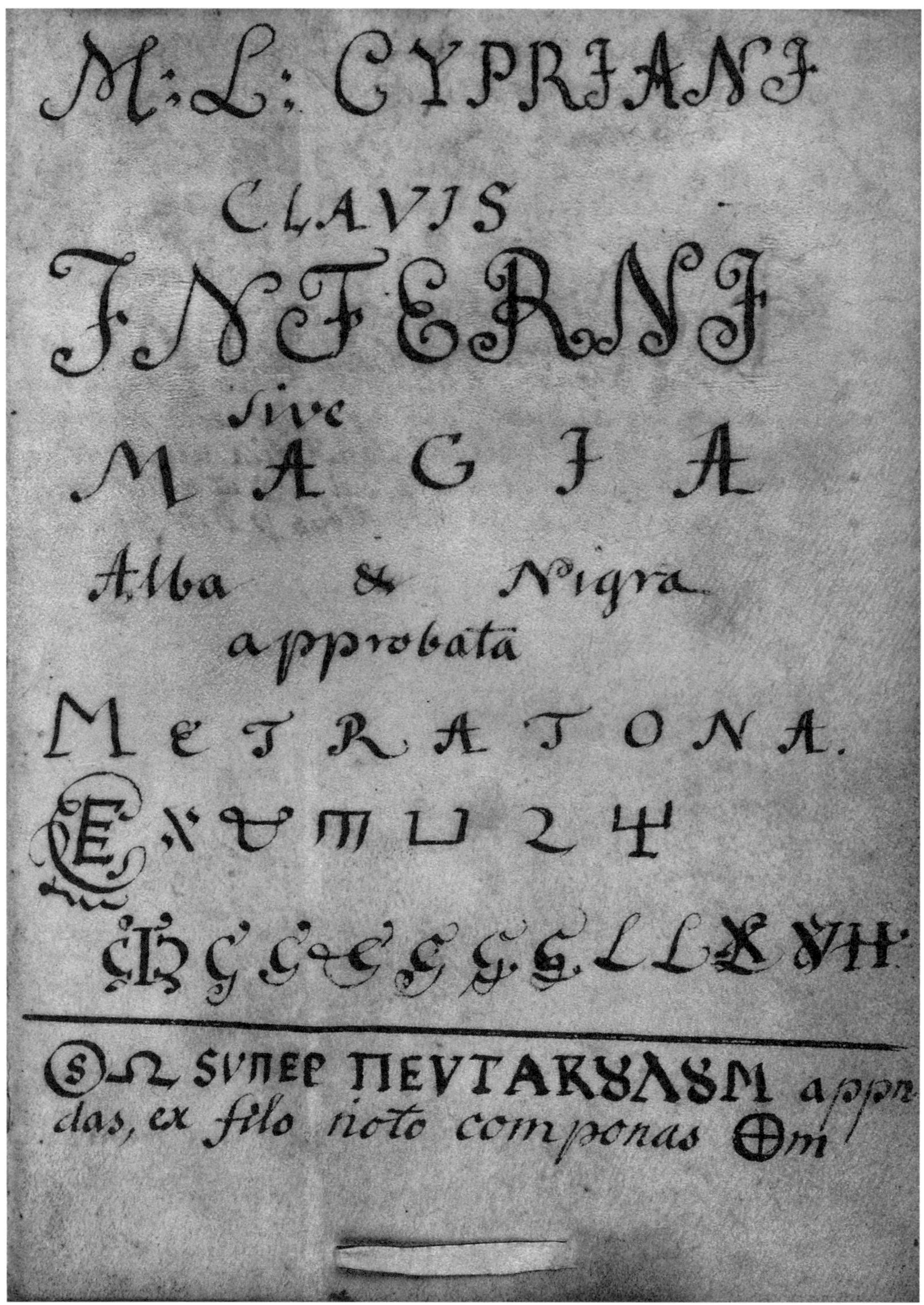

M: L: CYPRIANI

CLAVIS

INFERNI

sive

MAGIA

Alba & Nigra

approbata

METRATONA.

appen-
das, ex filo rioto componas

The title page of the *Clavis Inferni*.

[4]

Text:

M: L: CYPRIANI

CLAVIS
INFERNI

sive
MAGIA
Alba & Nigra

approbata
METRATONA.

(Abiruth?)

MCCCCCCLLXVII

S[anctus] Ω SUΠEP ΠENTAKΥΛΥΜ [1]
App[e]ndas, ex filo noto componas [oratione]m

Translation:

Magistri Ludi Cypriani [2]

A Key to Hell
and
Magic
White & Black

proven by
Metatron

A (Albiruth?)[3]

1757 [4]

Holy Spirit of the Pentacle appended,
from the string of notes compose a prayer [5]

---

[1] 'Pentakulum' does not appear in many Latin dictionaries, but means 'Pentacle'.

[2] Meaning '[the book] of the teacher Cyprianus'. The Mediaeval title 'Magister Ludi' was revived in Denmark in 1848.

[3] Probably the name of the author or compiler of this manuscript rendered in magical script.

[4] See the Introduction for more discussion of this date.

[5] This note probably applies to the Pentacle of the Holy Spirit on the previous page, rather than being part of the title page itself, hence the heavy ruled line above it. The prayer is presumably to the seven Archangels.

Figure 7: The Golden Seal.
[5]

The Golden Seal

This golden seal may have been intended as a lamen to be worn for the personal protection of the conjurer. At the top are the seals of the Archangels Michael and Gabriel, and at the bottom of the page the seals of Raphael and Sachiel.[1]

The Seal is an equilateral triangle containing a smaller inverted equilateral triangle. This is circumscribed by a circle, drawn in (faded) red on gold. Above the Seal are the letters A S A (the second A sigilised), and P G P at the bottom.

Between the circle and the triangle are the Hebrew words אלהינו ALHINV,[2] אראריתא ARARIThA, and אחד AChD. Inside the large triangle שדי ShDI (Shaddai) is repeated three times. In the middle triangle are permutations of the Tetragrammaton IHVH, וה הוה יהוה.[3]

---

[1] As shown in Agrippa's *Fourth Book of Occult Philosophy,* edited by Stephen Skinner, Ibis Press, Berwick, 2005, pages 76-85.

[2] This is a scribe's error, and it should read אלהים ALHIM not אלהינו ALHINV.

[3] Traces of Latin are left under the gilding from a previous text, including words like '[Ex]orcismus', indicating that the vellum had previously been used for a similar subject.

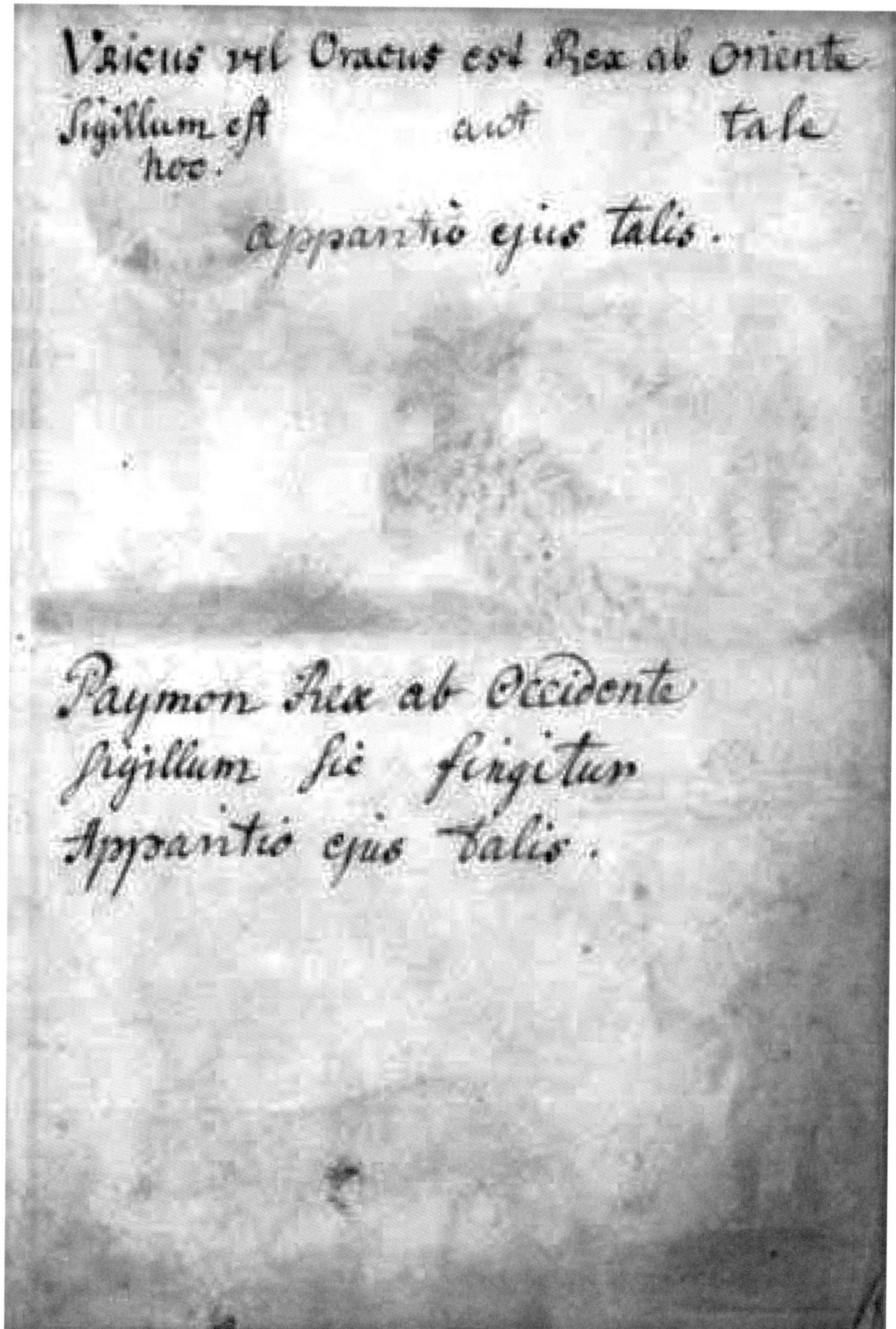

Vricus vel Oracus est Rex ab Oriente
Sigillum est hoc. aut tale
Apparitio ejus talis.

Paymon Rex ab Occidente
Sigillum sic fingitur
Apparitio ejus talis.

[6]

Urieus vel Uraeus est Rex ab Oriente
Sigillum est hoc aut tale
Apparitio ejus talis.

Paymon Rex ab Occidente
Sigillum Sic fingitur
Apparitio ejus talis,

Urieus or Uraeus is the King from the East
His seal is this or thus
His appearance is thus.

Paymon is the King from the West
His seal formed in this way
His appearance is thus.

Figure 8: The Demon Kings Urieus and Paymon.

Urieus (East) with a red winged Ouroboros is captioned MIKAL (Michael) IHVH. Paymon (West) is captioned RPAL (Raphael) ShDI (Shaddai). Both Demon Kings have a sceptre and a Seal. See Appendix I, Column L48.

[7]

Figure 9: The Demon Kings Maymon and Egyn.

The upper picture shows Maymon (South) in red with a bird and the caption is GBRIAL (Gabriel) HINV [ALHIM]. The lower picture shows Egyn (North) in blue with a bear-like creature and the caption is URIAL (Uriel) AChTh. Both Demon Kings have a sceptre and a Seal.

[8]

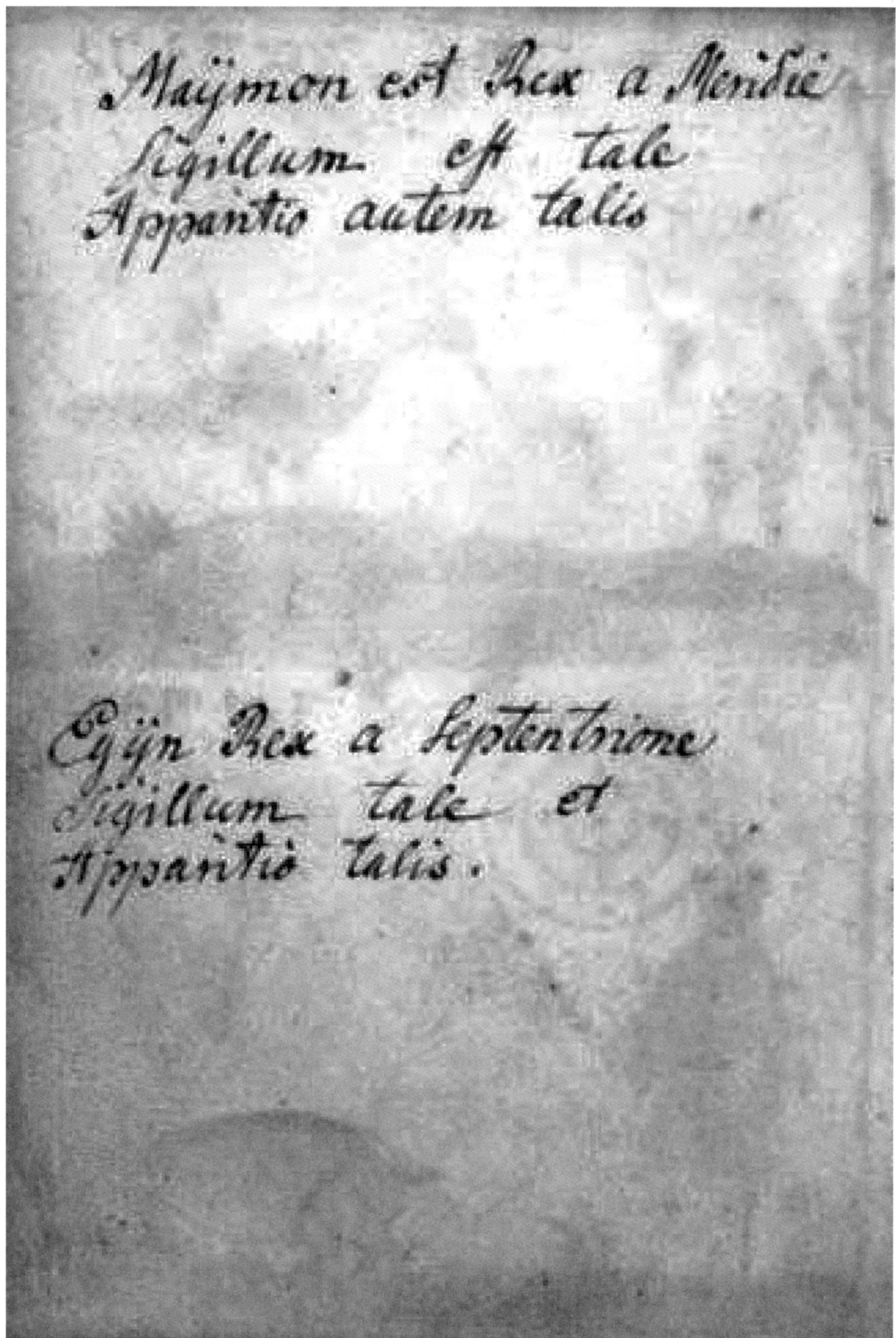

Maijmon est Rex a Meridie
Sigillum est tale
Apparitio autem talis

Egijn Rex a Septentrione
Sigillum tale et
Apparitio talis.

[9]

Maymon est Rex a Meridie

Sigillum est tale
Apparitio autem talis.

Egyn Rex a Septentrione
Sigillum tale e[s]t
Apparitio talis.

Maymon is the King of the South
His seal is thus
and his appearance thus.

Egyn is the King of the North
His seal [is] thus and
Appearance thus.

[Two further illustrations, the Vinculum Maximum and the Pentagram, appear at the end of the manuscript (unnumbered pages 20 and 21). We have moved these forward to this point, before the main text, in order to group all the illustrations together.]

Figure 10: The Vinculum Maximum.

[20]

The Vinculum Maximum literally means the 'greatest chain' or 'greatest bond'. In the centre is the Calvary cross entwined with the snake, set upon a skull and crossbones (representing the redemption of Adam's original sin). This is set upon a triangle (or pyramid). Behind this is a crossed sword and palm, denoting Christ as Warrior (as in *Revelation*) and as bringer of Peace (Palm Sunday). The pyramid is inscribed with three Hebrew yods י (the Trinity) and the Tetragrammaton (יהוה IHVH).

Beside this cross are the Hebrew godnames **אגלא** AGLA and **אדונאי** ADONAI, with the alchemical symbols for Saturn, and a composite sigil containing Mercury, Venus, Sun, Moon Mars and Jupiter. There is also a Libra-like sign showing the cross between Heaven and Earth.

The cross is embraced by a white crowned and winged Dragon (similar to the dragon which appears in the East with Urieus) devouring a black lizard.

At the top of the illustration is the Latin phrase *Vinculum Maximum,* which suggests that this image is probably to be used in binding the spirits. Underneath are the Greek letters A KAI Ω meaning 'alpha and omega' the beginning and the end. Libra and Θ lie below.

The Latin text underneath the dragon and lizard is *Qui facis Mirabilia magna Solus, Finis coronat opus,* which means 'You who alone perform great wonders, the end crowns the work'.[1]

On the left hand side is the Greek text *o theos agiotatos esti o megistos plutos* meaning "God is most holy, the [giver of] greatest wealth".

On the right hand side is the matching Greek text: *o kyrios* [sigilised A] *ton panton pnei* which means "The Lord A moves upon everything".[2] The sigilised 'A' might indicate Adonai, or maybe some other darker Lord.

---

[1] From the *Psalter*: "O omnipotens sempiterne Deus, qui facis mirabilia magna solus: prætende super famulos tuos pontifices, et super cunctas congregationes illis commissas, spiritum gratias salutaris: et ut in veritate tibi complaceant, perpetuum eis rorem tuæ benedidtionis infunde."—*Brev. Saris. Psalter,* Paris, 1556, folio lx, page 2.

[2] These Greek passages contain serious syntax errors, and therefore confirm that the scribe was not fluent in that language, or indeed in Hebrew either.

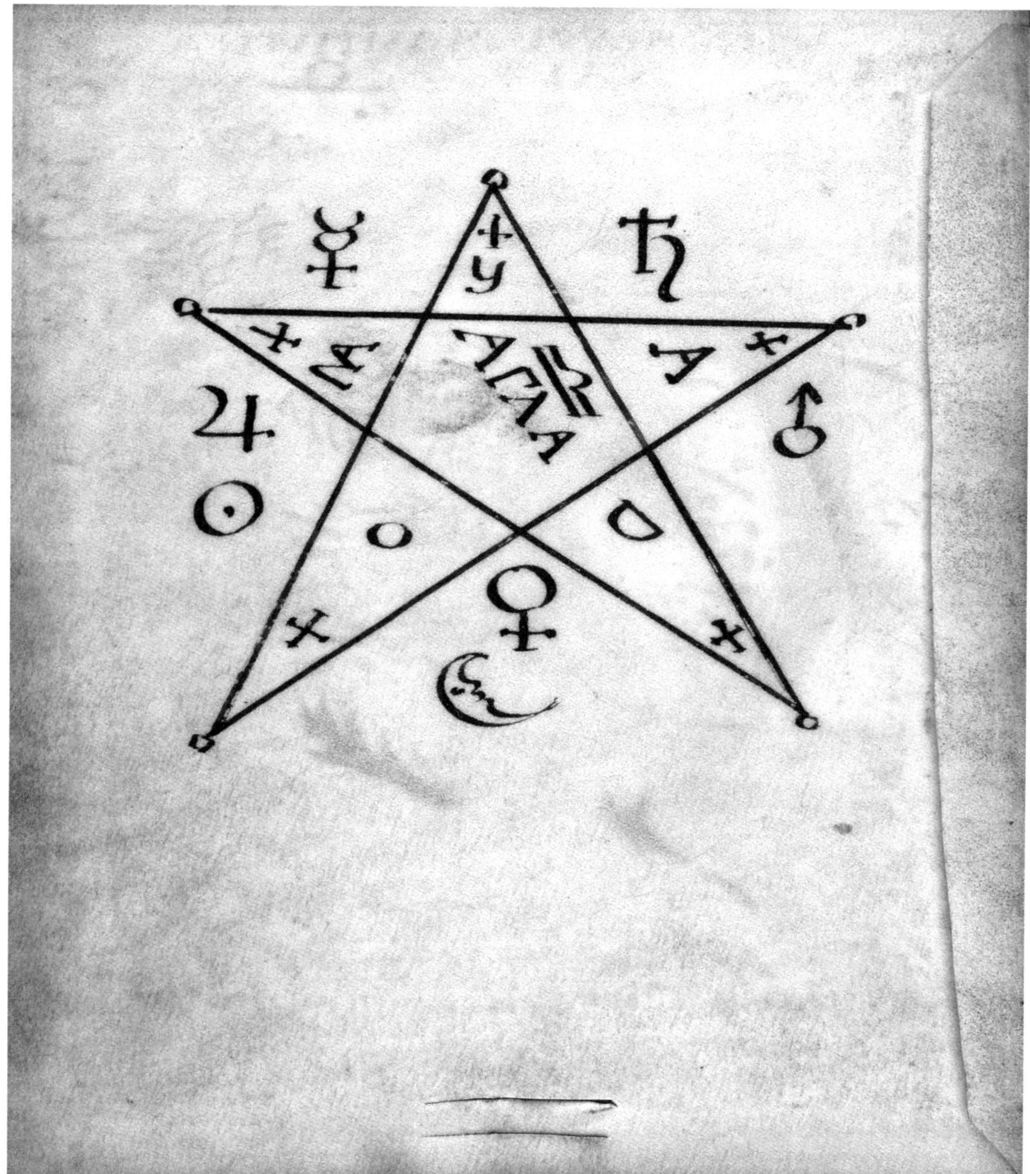

Figure 11: The Pentagram Seal.

The Pentagram has Libra and AΓΛA (AGLA) inscribed in the centre. A-D-O-NA-Y (ADONAY the Hebrew for 'Lord') appears in the vertices. The 7 planets Saturn, Mars, Venus & Moon, Sun & Jupiter, and Mercury are inscribed between the vertices in a clockwise direction. The two slits for the parchment tongue used to close the book can be clearly seen at the bottom.

Nota: omnia sub Dio I vice fiant, inque manu sinistra hunc teneas librum, Dextrae vero manus III digitos Priores arrigas. dicens:

EXCLAMATIO.

Ego N.N. Pa D Dttg ozizroxe sov.. N.N
e fundo totiq Idnum Silanrefni. & retentnet
op p na A V & VR D orefomi p etrof. &
elibarimda Sא אלהים, אדוני, צבוה, tu Sitarea-
pppa cih atxui Mulucric in pulchra forma
visibili humana, & enis. etatis outro ♀
aqila, etinv quia vobis impero p ●
אליון, יהוה, שדי, אל, יה,
אלוה, אראריתא, יהשוה, אלהים
ורצה, אלהים גיבר, sov ocov
p □es Coelos, Chrbm & Arphm, ♀r
ns Dntns et universas Ttsts, atque Vr-
tts ✠✠✠ Clmntes, IV. ⊙ Ttts MΓP
& ✹ & ☽ & ⊡ ✶s ш ⩚ ⊖ ☽ Aesttm
Vrm Hmm Amm & □e qd laudat M.N.
⊖ D. Ei super □a. B. atqp SSS. Mrsi
M Fssi, Us, Mrahassi. M. R Laudabilissimi Xs Invincibilis, Creatoris
⊙ & ☽ [V] Incarnati, et Tragas.
Anti ⊖ ☋ Amen.

[10]

Sinite igitur [symbol] [symbol] illos res
erinev cuh ni Ne Θ Esi Sabaoth
Regis Regum Pssi. ne differatis
erinev [symbol] adudācsifirotq ineffabile Nomen Θ Creatoris Sapientissimi [symbol] D. Nostri ! Cuius Nn
enis enif laudabile !

Quoniam Ego N.N. vos giur□ [symbol]
□e quod ✝ in [symbol] & ☽ p Sedem
Baldachia, virtute Nominis [symbol]
nevnalor vobis pertinacissimis
inobedientibus, □ibq Vribq ☉ &
☽ ocidelam & ovirp sov oi ocol
& oiduag evqsu ni muidnuforp,
issyba et usqz ad mumitlu
meid iicidui sov ogeler ni ge
men ◎ atque in manga [symbol] ♀ [symbol]
& [symbol] imo vos tegnup suidalg
cari Θ Omnipotentis et Iustissi-
mi Iudicis Trementissimi et
Invincibilis Emanuelis mei
isin mitast sitacrappa cih
atxui mulucric itatnulov eam

[11]

irutcaßsitas, selibibiv & selibassa
ni archlup amrof venite ergo
in nomine SSS Bssi ac Treme-
tissimi Θ צבות ארוני festinate
imperat sibov ℞ muger Sx. Aty
Titeip, Azia, Hyn, IenMinosel, A=
chadan, vay, vaa, Eij, Haa, Eije,
Exe, a El, El, El, a Hy. Hau. Hau
Hau, va, va, va, va,

Ter Dicito.
Amorule, Taneha, Latisten, Rabur
Taneha, Latisten, Escha, Aladia,
Α & Ω Laiste oniston, Adonai,
Clementissime Ptr miserere mei
Peccatoris, indigni filii tui, et Clarifica in me Tuæ Ptntiæ Brachium, gtra hos Ω Mtnessmes, ut ego
possim adorare et glorificare Nu
Tuum ✠ ✠ ✠, supplex te invoco
ut tuo Ideo hi Ω quos voco qvcti
et gstreti veniant vocati, Postulat
nbg siem irutcaßsitas non fremen
tes non setnerret cen setnedal son

[12]

des ni oibg tnis sibon setneidebo
p Jesum Xstum Filium tuum
atque Ω Παρχκλητον Amen.

Citatio.

Ego N.N. otic & ooov et mepicnirp
Ω N.N. ut jam mihi appareas in
Specie humana celeriter et citatim
p Nn Ineffabile יהוה Creatons oūi
A V & Vi Θi, Angelos Ms MPΓ
♉ & □a q3 +a sunt in ☉ & ☽ pra
cipio vobis ut ihim muruacht
Ⲁ Ⲁ ♄ ☉ xe ♒ extrahas ostendas
et tradas in Ne D Bathat vel vachat
sup Abrac ruens supvenienssntocor
sup Aberer, advenias hucusque
hactenus horsum-ante huncce
rnulucric in quo sum jam in ♉

4 ☉ ☿ ♀ ☽

Protinus, continuo, tantumodo,
fac Tu quod volo abs Te et Ego
vicissim faciam quod Hanorem

[13]

D Θ X invincibilis Emanuelis mei
multiplicat Amen Amen Amen

Conjuratio
ter dicatur.

Conjuro te Ω Inferni NN per to=
tam universitatem ejus tartari
in quo mansionem tuam habes
ut mihi jam apparcas, et Te Imperio meo submittas, quo p Θ □ M Cre.
atorem ☉ & ☽ sum dits, omneq
Obsequium praestans impleas vo.
luntatem meam in Citatione praemissa expressam, per α & ω ❖ VY
אדוני, אחד, אלהינו, יהוה, אל, M.
Γ. P. 8 appare ergo virtute nominum Aye Saraye, Aye Saraye,
Aye Saraye, ne differas pervenire
per Nomina Aeterna Θi V & Vi
Eloy, Archima, Rabur, cui sit
Laus Honor et gloria in aeternum
Amen.

[14]

Vinculum & Allocutio.

Ego N.N. ligo et vinculo te Ω N. p hanc horam hoc loco dia lor Θεὸν Patrem & Filium, & Spiritum Sanctum et per Novem Ordines Angelorum, Salvete ergo Ω quia vos vocavi per illum cui omne genu flectitur, coelestium Terrestrium, et Infernorum, cuius in manu omnia regna Regum sunt, nec est qui suae contrarius esse possit Majestati, quatenus nunc constringo vos ut hic ante Circulum visibiles et affabiles permaneatis, tamdiu tamque constantes nec sine permissione et licentia recedatis, donec meam sine fallacia aliqua et veridice perficiatis voluntatem.

[15]

per Potentia illius virtutem qui Mari posuit Terminum suum, quem preterire non potest, et lege illius Potentia non pertransit fines suos. Dei, Altissimi, Regis, Domini, qui cuncta creavit Amen.

Ter repete

Fuga Dæmonum

Audi Tu ad verba mea mihi obediens et voluntatem meam explere consuete Ω. N.N. abi jam rursus in locum tuum ubi fuisti antequam Te advocavi huc donec Ego Volente Deo Te iterum vocavero, sisq; semp paratus venire vocatus p nomi Vivi & Veri, & Invincibilis Dei Trementissimi atq; Fortissi

[16]

mi, Ego vero ex Lege illius
Majestatis Thesaurum in Citatione præmissa postulatum
abs te accipio et auffero; Abi
nunc Placatissime in locum tuum sine rumore, Tumultu et
sine læsione nostruum et circuli aliorumque hominum, in
Nomine Patris + et Fi-
lii + & Spiritus Sancti +
A M E N.

IHS

[17]

Tunc Scribito.
S. A. I I R I V I D S T N
9tra omne M C & A.

Dimissio scribatur
VX III Um Um W X. Ч Witt@
VXS III I ɔ ⊙ Ш VЧ N @ W III
ЧV ≠ X Λ I a quoquam, VX°V
ч ш Ч ђ ≁ ₲ ϴ T U X.
+ ☉ + Meotorile + + Lei + Pelei +
Jonar + Jonar + Psui +
+ offstam. +

J + L

[18]

[*The transcription of the main text of the manuscript now follows, in pairs of facing pages, with the Latin, Greek, Hebrew and magical scripts on the left, and the English translation on the right. The left hand page displays two texts: the original and an expanded version*]

Text

[p. 10]

Nota: Omnia Sub Dio I[n]vice[m] fiant, inque manu sinistra hunc teneas librum, Dextrie vero manus III digitos Priores arrigos. dicens:

EXCLAMATIO

Ego NN. [Nomen] Pa[ter] [Domini] D[o]t[a]t[um] ozicrexe sov[1] Ω[2] [Spiritus] NN [Nomen] è fundo toti[us] [3] Idnum Silanrefni, & retentnetop p[er] n[omin]a [aeturnum] [vivi] & [veri] [Domini] orepmi p[er] etrof & elibarimda אל. אלהים. אדוני. צבות tu sitaerappa cih atxui Mulucric in pulchra forma visibili humana,[4] & enis etatisoutro[t] a[u]qila, etineu quia vobis impero p[er] י. יה. אל. שדי. יהוה. אליון. אלהים. יהשוה. אראריתא. אלוה ודצת. גיבר אלהים...

Expansion:

Nota: Omnia Sub Dio Invicem fiant, inque manu sinistra hunc teneas librum, dextrie vero manus tres digitos Priores arrigos, dicens:

EXCLAMATIO

Ego NN. [Nomen] Pater Domini Dotatum exorcizo vos Spiritus NN [Nomen] è fundo totius Mundi Infernalis & potentneter per nomina aeturnum vivi & veri Domini impero per forte & admirabile AL, ALHIM, ADONI, TzBVTh ut appareatis hic juxta Circulum in pulchra forma visibili humana, & sine tortuositate aliqua, uenite quia vobis impero per I, IH, AL, ShDI, IHVH, ALION, ALHIM, IHShVH, ARARIThA, ALVH VDTzTh,[5] GIBR ALHIM...[6]

---

[1] The red text indicates Latin words that have been reversed in the original, and which are then re-ordered in the Expansion at the lower half of each left hand page.

[2] Ω and Σ indicate 'Spiritus' or spirit (in the sense of demon, not in the sense of spiritual).

[3] The '9' shaped character is in fact a Latin contraction mark for '-us' if used as the final syllable, or for 'con-' if used at the front of a word.

[4] Cf. Peter de Abano, *Heptameron*: ut appareatis statim nobis hic juxta circulum in pulchra forma, videlicet humana, et sine deformitate.

[5] An error in the original Hebrew ודצת. It should be ודעת VDOTh, i.e Eloah va-Daath.

[6] Cf. *Heptameron*: Exorcismus spirituum aereorum: Nos facti ad imaginem Dei, & ejus facti voluntate, per potentissimum & corroboratum nomen Dei El, forte & admirabile vos exorcizamus & imperamus per eum qui dixit, & factum est, & per omnia nomina Dei, & per nomen Adonay, El, Elohim, Elohe, Zebaoth, Elion, Escerchie, Jah, Tetragrammaton, Sadai, Dominus Deus, excelsus, exorcizamus vos, atque potenter imperamus, ut appareatis statim nobis hic juxta Circulum in pulchra forma, videlicet humana, & sine deformitate & tortuositate aliqua.

Translation

Note: All things are subject to the power of the Divine, and are done one after the other, [so] let you hold this book in the left hand, and with the right hand, the first three fingers raised, say:

CALLING[1]

I [Name],[2] [in the name of the] Father and Lord powerfully exorcise you Spirit [Name] from the bottom of the whole Infernal World, & powerful through the name of the ever-living and true Lord, I powerfully command you through the strong and wonderful [names] El, Elohim, Adonai, Tzabaoth, that you appear before this Circle in a fair visible human form, & without tortuosity, come because I command you through [the names] I, Yah, El, Shaddai, IHVH, Elion, Elohim, Yeheshuah,[3] Ararita, Eloah va-Daath, Elohim Gibor…[4]

---

[1] Literally 'to shout, or to call alound by name.'

[2] Your name.

[3] IHShVH or יהשוה is a Christian Kabbalistic name for Christ consisting of the Hebrew letter ש Shin inserted into the middle of the Hebrew Tetragramaton יהוה IHVH. It originated in Johann Reuchlin's *De Verbo Mirifico, On the Wonder-working Word* (1494) as part of his program to use the Kabbalah to help convert the Jews to Christianity. This form IHShVH was adopted by Heinrich Khunrath in his Sigillum Dei Aemeth in *Amphitheatrum Sapientiae Aeternae, Amphitheatre of Eternal Wisdom* (1609).

[4] Cf. *The Magical Ritual of the Sanctum Regnum*: "By the great names, Araritha, Eloah va Daath, Elohim Tzabaoth and Elohim Gibur, may this water be consecrated for the service of those who are about to invoke the Divine Powers for the benefit of their souls. Amen."

Text

[p. 10 continued]

...sov ocov p[er] [r]es Coelos, Ch[e]r[u]b[i]m & [S][e]r[a]ph[i]m, [T][h]r[o]n[e]s D[omi]n[a]t[io]ns et universas Π[o]t[e]st[e]s, atque V[i]rt[u]t[e]s +++ Cl[e]m[e]ntes, IV [Coelos] Π[rince]Πs Μ Γ Ρ Υ [Sol] & [Luna] & [volvere?] [Sidu]s Terra Ignis Aqua Aer Æst[a]t[e]m V[e]rn[um] H[ye]m[e]m A[utu]m[nu]m & [r]e q[uo]d laudat M.N. [Dei] [Domini] Ꝭi[?] super [r]a. Benedicti atq[ue] SSS [Sacrosanctissimi]. M[i]r[u]s[?] I [Raphael], F[orti]ssi[mi], [Gabriel], M[ichael] par L[abili]ssi, [Aeternum], [Haniel], Laudabilissimi [Tzadkiel]. Invincibilis, Creatoris [Sol] & [Luna] [Christ][1] Incarnati, et *Παρακλητι* [Dei] [Triunus], Amen.

Expansion

...vos voco per res Coelos, Cherubim & Seraphim, Thrones, Dominationes, et universas Potestes, atque Virtutes +++ Clementes 4 Coelos Princeps Michael, Gabriel, Raphael, Uriel; Sol & Luna & [volvere] Sidus; Terra, Ignis, Aqua, Aer; Æstatem Vernum Hyemem Autumnum & re quod laudat M. N. Dei Domini Ꝭi super ra Benedictus, atque Sacrosanctissimi Mirus I Raphael, Fortissimi Gabriel, Michael par Labilissi, Aeternum Haniel, Laudabilissimi Tzadkiel. Invincibilis Creatoris Sol & Luna, Christ Incarnati, et Paraklete Dei tripartitus, Amen.

[1] This symbol may also have been used for Tzaphkiel, but here it can only refer to the second person of the Trinity.

Translation

...I call you through the Heavens, the Cherubim & Seraphim, Thrones, Dominations and Universal Powers and Virtues[1] +++[2] and the merciful four chiefs of the heavens: Michael, Gabriel, Raphael, and Uriel; the Sun and Moon & revolving Stars; [the Elements] Earth, Fire, Water, Air; Summer, Spring, Winter, Autumn, & that praises M. N. Lord God Ɫi set above the Blessed and most Sacrosanct wonderful Raphael; strong Gabriel; redeeming Michael; eternal Haniel; praiseworthy Tzadkiel. Invincible Creator of the Sun and Moon, Christ Incarnate, and the Paraclete,[3] the Triune God, Amen.

---

[1] These are the different hierarchies of angels.

[2] Here the Operator should make the sign of the cross.

[3] *Paraclete* in Koine Greek (the language of the Septuagint and the New Testament) means a 'helper' or 'comforter', or 'someone who is called in'. See *John* 14:16. It also sometimes refers to the Holy Spirit. In Classical Greek there is a sense where the Paraclete is portrayed as the 'defence advocate' opposing the 'accuser' (or *diabolus*) at the trial of the soul.

Text

[p. 11]
Sinite igitur ◫ ◙ illos res erineu cuh ni N[omin]e [Dei] Esi Sabaoth Regis Regnum P[otenti]ssi[mi], ne differatis erineu Ω [Spiritus] ad[n]u d[n]acifirolg ineffabile Nomen [Dei] Creatoris Sapientissimi [Benedicti] D[omini] Nostri! Cuius N[ome]n enis enif laudabile!

Expansion

Sinite igitur [clavis inferni?][1] illos res venire huc in Nomine Dei Esi Sabaoth Regis Regnum Potentissimi, ne differatis venire[2] Spiritus glorifica[n]d unda ineffabile Nomen Dei Creatoris Sapientissimi Benedicti Domini Nostri! Cuius Nomen sine fine laudabile!

---

[1] We have not deciphered these two characters, but on the basis that the second one bears a passing resemblance to medieval pictures of the mouth of hell, it is possible that this character could be translated as 'inferni'. This interpretation is far from certain, but if this is the case then it provides some justification for the title of the manuscript.

[2] *Heptameron*: ne differatis venire.

Translation

Therefore allow the key of hell [to open][1] that place, come here in the Name of God Esi Tzabaoth, most Powerful King of Kings, do not defer to come Spirit by the glory of the ineffable Name of God, the Wisest Creator our Blessed Lord! Whose name is to be praised without end!

---

[1] A very speculative translation.

Text

[p. 11 continued]
Quoniam Ego NN. vos [con]i[u]ro [Princeps?]. [r]e quod + in [IX Coelos] & [Luna] p[er] Sedem Baldachiae, virtute Nominis Πριμευματον vobis pertinacissimis, inobedientibus, [r]ibus v[i]rib[us] [Sol] & [Luna] ocidelam & ovirp sov oi ocol & oiduag euqsu ni mudnuforp[ro] issyba et usq[ue] ad mumitlu meid [m]ü[i]cidui sov ogeler ni gi-men ◉ atque in munga♀☿ ⏊ & ♀ i[n]mo vos tegnup suidalg aeri [Dei] Omnipotentis et Justissimi Judicis Trementissimi et Invincibilis Emanuelis mei isin mitast sitaerappa cih atxui mulucric itatnulov eaem [p. 12] irutcafsitas, selibisiv & selibassa ni archlup amrof venite ergo in nomine SSS B[enedicti]ssi[mus] ac Trementissimi [Dei] צבות ארוני festinate imperat sibov ℞ muger אל. Aty, Titeip, Azia, Hyn, Ien, Minosel, Achadan, vay, vaa, Ey, Haa, Eye, Exe, a El, El, El, a Hy, Hau, Hau, Hau, va, va, va, va.[1]

Expansion:

Quoniam Ego N.N. vos conjuro Princeps re quod + in IX Coelos & Luna per Sedem Baldachiae, virtute Nominis Primeumaton [2] vobis pertinacissimis, inobedientibus,[3] ribus viribus Sol & Luna maledico & privo vos o[mn]i loco & gaudio usque in profundum abyssi et usque ad ultimum diem judicium vos relego in ignem [aeternum] atque in [st]agnum [terra] & [sulphuris] omni vos punget gladius irae Dei Omnipotentis et Justissimi Judicis Tremendissimi et Invincibilis Emanuelis mei nisi statim appareatis hic juxta circulum voluntati meae [p. 12] satisfacturi, visibiles & affabiles in pulchra forma venite ergo in nomine Sacrosanctissimi Benedictissimus ac Trementissimi Dei ADONI TzBVTh, festinate imperat vobis Haniel regum AL, Aty, Titeip, Azia, Hyn, Ien, Minosel, Achadan, vay, vaa, Ey, Haa, Eye, Exe, a, El, El, El, a, Hy, Hau, Hau, Hau, va, va, va, va.[4]

---

[1] *Heptameron*: Adonay, Saday, Rex regum, El, Aty, Titeip, Azia, Hyn, Jen, Minosel, Achadan: Vay, Vaa, Ey, Haa, Eye, Exà , Ee, l, El, El, à , Hy, Hau, Hau, Hau, Va, Va, Va , Va.

[2] *Heptameron*: per sedem Baldachia, et per hoc nomen Primeumaton…et in virtute istius nominis Primeumaton.

[3] *Heptameron*: vobis pertinacissimis.

[4] *Heptameron*: & in virtute istius nominis Primeumaton, tota Coeli militia compellente, maledicimus vos, privamus vos omni officio, loco & gaudio vestro, esque in profundum abyssi, & usque ad ultimum diem judicii vos ponimus, & relegamus in ignem æternum, & in stagnum ignis & sulphuris, nisi statim appareatis hic coram nobis, inte Circulum, ad faciendum voluntatem nostram. In omnibus venite per hæc nomina, Adonay Zebaoth, Adonay, Amioram. Venite, venite, imperat vobis Adonay, Saday, Rex regum potentissimus & tremendissimus, cujus vires nulla subterfugere potest creatura vobis pertinacissimis futuris nisi obedieritis, & appareatis ante hunc Circulum, affabiles subito, tandem ruina flebilis miserabilisque, & ignis perpetuum inextinguibilis vos manet. Venite ergo in nomine Adonay Zebaoth, Adonay Amioram: venite, venite, quid tardatis? festinate imperat vobis Adonay, Saday, Rex regum, El, Aty, Titeip, Azia, Hyn, Jen, Minosel, Achadan: Vay, Vaa, Ey, Haa, Eye, Exe, à, El, El, El, à, Hy, Hau, Hau, Hau, Va, Va, Va, Va.

Translation

Since I [Name] conjure you Prince [of Spirits] again that + is in the Ninth Heaven & the Moon in the seat of the Baldachiæ,[1] by the virtue of the Name Primeumaton, you most obstinate, inobedient powers of the Sun & Moon, I curse and deprive you of all place [in Heaven] and joy, and I banish you to eternal fire and the depths of the abyss, [below] the earth in brimstone till the day of the last judgement. And may the sword of wrath of the Almighty God, the Most Just Judge, the most dreadful and Invincible Emanuel, afflict you unless you immediately appear before this circle to satisfy my wish, visible and affable in a fair form, come therefore in the most sacrosanct, praiseworthy and dreadful name of God, Adonai Tzabaoth, hurry, Haniel commands you, El, Aty, Titeip, Azia, Hyn, Ien, Minosel, Achadan, vay, vaa, Eij, Haa, Eije, Exe, a El, El, El, a Hy, Hau, Hau, Hau, va, va, va, va.[2]

---

[1] A baldachia is a canopy over the altar, so it is a poetic phrase likening the Moon to that canopy.

[2] Note this phrase occurs in the *Heptameron* and also in Faust, *Magia Naturalis et Innaturalis.* See Figure 1.

Text

[p. 12 continued]
Ter Dicito

Amorule, Taneha, Latisten, Rabur, Taneha, Latisten, Escha, Aladia, A & Ω Leiste Oriston, Adonai, Clementissime P[a]t[e]r miserere mei Peccatoris, indigni filii tui, et Clarifica in me Tuæ P[o]t[e]ntiae Brachium, [con]tra hos Ω Π[e]ρt[ici]n[aci]ss[i]mos, ut ego possim adorare et glorificare N[ome]n Tuum +++, supplex te invoco ut tuo I[u]d[i]c[i]o hi Ω quos voco [con]u[i]cti et [con]stri[c]ti veniant vocati, Postulationib[us] siem irutcafsitas non frementes non setnerret cen setnedael son [p. 13] des ni oib[us] tnis sibon setneidebo per Jesum [Chri]stum Filium tuum atque Ω Παρακλετον, Amen.[1]

Expansion

Ter Dicito

Amorule, Taneha, Latisten, Rabur, Taneha, Latisten, Escha, Aladia, Alpha & Omega, Leiste Oriston, Adonai, Clementissime Pater miserere mei Peccatoris, indigni filii tui, et Clarifica in me Tuæ Potentiae Brachium contra hos Spiritus perticinacissimos, ut ego possim adorare et glorificare Nomen Tuum +++, supplex te invoco ut tuo Judicio hi Spiritus quos voco conuicti et constricti veniant vocati, Postulationibus meis satisfacturi non frementes non terrentes nec laedentes nos [p. 13] sed in subi[t]o sint nobis obedientes per Jesum Christum Filium tuum atque Spiritus Parakleton, Amen.

---

[1] Cf. *Heptameron*: "A Morule, Taneha, Latisten, Rabur, Taneha, Latisten, Escha, Aladia, Alpha & Omega, Leyste, Oriston, Adonay: Clementissime pater mi cœlestis, miserere mei, licet peccatoris, clarifica in me hodierno die, licet indigno filio tuo tuæ potentiæ brachium, contra hos spiritus perticinacissimos: vt ego, te volente, factus tuorum diuinorum operum contemplator, possim illustirari omni sapientia, & semper glorificare & adorare nomen tuum. Suppliciter exoro te, & invoco, vt tuo iudicio hi spiritus: quos invoco, convicti & constricti, veniant vocati & dent vera responsa, de quibus eos interrogauero: dentq; & deferant nobis ea quæ per me vel nos præcipietur eis, non nocentes alicui creaturæ, non lædentes, non frementes, nec me sociósque meos vel aliam creaturam lædentes, & neminem terrentes: sed petitionibus meis, in omnibus quæ præcipiam eis, sint obedientes."

Translation

Say Three Times

Amorule, Taneha, Latisten, Rabur, Taneha, Latisten, Escha, Aladia, Alpha & Omega, Leiste, Oriston, Adonai,[1] O my most Merciful Father, have mercy upon my sins, your unworthy son, and make appear the Arm of thy Power in me this day against this most obstinate Spirit, so that I might adore and glorify your Name +++, humbly I call upon your judgement that this Spirit which I call may come subdued and constrained to answer my questions satisfactorily, not raging, nor terrifying or harming us, but may he be rapidly obedient to us in all things, through Jesus Christ your Son, and the Spirit of the Paraclete, Amen.

[1] *Heptameron*: A Morule, Taneha, Latisten, Rabur, Taneha, Latisten. Escha, Aladia, Alpha & Omega, Leyste, Oriston, Adonay.

Text

Citatio

Ego NN otic & ocov et mepicnirp Ω NN ut jam mihi appareas in specie humana celeriter et citatim per N[ome]n Ineffabile יהוה Creatoris ou[m] [aeternum] [vivi] & [veri] [Dei], Angelos M[undi?] S[anctus?] MPΓϒ & [r]a q[uam] +a sunt in [Sol] & [Luna] praecipio vobis ut ihim muruaseht ⩚ ⩛ ꟾ♭ [Sol] xe [aqua] extrahas ostendas et tradas in N[omin]e [Domini] Bathat vel Vachat sup[er] Abrac ruens superveniens Abeor sup[er] Aberer,[1] advenias hucusque hactenus horsum ante huncce mulucric in quo sum jam in ⧗

Protinus, continuo, tantum[m]odo, fac Tu quod volo abs Te et Ego vicissim faciam quod Honorem [p. 14] D[omini] [Dei] [omnipotens] invincibilis Emanuelis mei multiplicat Amen Amen Amen.

Expansion

Citatio

Ego NN cito & voco te principem Spiritus NN ut jam mihi appareas in specie humana celeriter et citatim per Nomen Ineffabile IHVH Creatoris oum aeternum vivi & veri Dei, Angelos Mundi Sanctus Michael Raphael Gabriel Uriel & ra quam +a sunt in Sol & Luna praecipio vobis ut mihi thesaurum ⩚ ⩛ ꟾ♭ Sol ex aqua extrahas ostendas et tradas in Nomine Domini Bathat vel Vachat super Abrac ruens superveniens Abeor super Aberer, advenias hucusque hactenus horsum ante huncce circulum in quo sum jam in hora

Iovis Sol Mercurius Venus Luna

Protinus, continuo, tantummodo, fac Tu quod volo abs Te et Ego vicissim faciam quod Honorem [p. 14] Domini Dei omnipotens invincibilis Emanuelis mei multiplicat Amen Amen Amen.

[1] *Heptameron*: in nomine Domini Bathat, vel Vachat super Abrac ruens, super veniens, Abeor super Aberer.

Translation

Summoning

I [Name] summon and call you chief Spirit NN [Name] that you may now quickly and immediately appear in human shape through the ineffable Name of Jehovah, the Creator, the Everliving and True God, and the chief angels of this holy world Michael, Raphael, Gabriel, Uriel, & are in the Sun and Moon, I enjoin you to extract, show and hand over to me the treasure ⩓ ⩓ ♭ gold from the waters, in the Name of the Lord Bathat or Vachat rushing upon Abrac, overcoming Aberer, and that you may come here to this place hither [before] this circle in which I now am in this hour [of]

Jupiter   Sun   Mercury   Venus   Moon[1]

Forthwith, immediately and as quickly as possible, do what I wish of you, and I in turn shall do honour to my [p. 14] Lord God Almighty, the invincible Emanuel, and may it multiply,[2] Amen, Amen, Amen.

---

[1] The five positive planets, leaving out the two malefics. These indicate that the correct planetary hour is chosen for the working, but the hours of Mars and Saturn are not included.

[2] Be successful.

Text

Conjuratio
ter dicatur

Conjuro te Ω Inferni NN [Nomen] per totam universitatem ejus tartari in quo mansionem tuam habes ut mihi jam appareas, et Te Imperio meo submittas, quo p[er] [Dei] R[egnare et] M[agnus] Creatorem [Sol] & [Luna] sum d[e]d[i]t[u]s, omneq[uam] obsequium praestans impleas voluntatem meam in Citatione praemissa expressam, per *α* & *ω* ׳ VY, אדוני, אחד, אלהימ[1]: יהוה, אל, ΜΓΡΥ appare ergo virtute nominum Aye Saraye, Aye Saraye, Aye Saraye, ne differas pervenire per Nomina Aeterna D[omin]i [vivi] & [veri] Eloy, Archima, Rabur, cui sit Laus, Honor, et Gloria in aeternum Amen.

Expansion

Conjuratio ter dicatur

Conjuro te Spiritus Inferni NN [Nomen] per totam universitatem ejus tartari in quo mansionem tuam habes ut mihi jam appareas, et Te Imperio meo submittas, quo per Dei Regnare et Magnus Creatorem Sol & Luna sum deditus, omnequam obsequium praestans impleas voluntatem meam in Citatione praemissa expressam, per alpha & omega, I, Vy, ADONI, AChAD, ALHIM, IHVH, AL, Michael, Gabriel, Raphael, Uriel appare ergo virtute nominum Aye Saraye, Aye Saraye, Aye Saraye, ne differas pervenire per Nomina Aeterna Domini vivi & veri Eloy, Archima, Rabur,[2] cui sit Laus, Honor, et Gloria in aeternum, Amen.

---

[1] The original Hebrew is miswritten as נו but should of course be ם.

[2] Cf. *Heptameron*: "Venite ergo cum festinatione in virtute nominum istorum, Aye, Saraye, Aye, Saraye, Aye Saraye, ne differatis venire, per nomina æterna Dei vivi & veri Dei vivi & veri Eloy, Archima, Rabur."

Translation

Conjuration to be said thrice

I conjure you Infernal spirit [Name] through the whole entirety of that Tartarus in which you have your dwelling that you appear now to me, and I command that you submit to me, who through the Ruling and Great God, the Creator of the Sun and Moon, [to whom] I am devoted, and waiting upon every indulgence, you may grant the wish I expressed in the summoning beforesaid, though alpha and omega, I, Vy, Adonai, Achad, Alhim, IHVH, El, Michael, Gabriel, Raphael, Uriel appear therefore by the virtue of the names Aye Saraye, Aye Saraye, Aye Saraye, do not defer to come through the Eternal Names of the living and true Lord Eloy, Archima, Rabur, to whom may there be praise, honour and glory for ever, Amen.

Text

[p. 15]

Vinculum & Allocutio

Ego NN ligo et vinculo te Ω N p[er] hunc horam hoc loco *δια του θεου*[1] Patrem & Filium, & Spiritum Sanctum et per novem ordines Angelorum, salvete ergo Ω quia vos vocavi per illum cui omne genu flectitur, Coelestium, Terrestrium, et Infernorum, cuius in manu omnia regna Reg[n]um sunt, nec est qui suae contrarius esse possit Majestati, quate[r]nus nunc constringo vos ut hic ante Circulum visibiles et affabiles permaneatis, tamdiu tamque constantes, nec sine permissione et licentia recidatis, donec meam sine fallacia aliqua et veridice perficiatis voluntatem, [p. 16] per Potentiæ illius virtutem qui Mare posuit Terminum suum, quem praeterire non potest, et lege illius Potentiae non pertransit fines suos, Dei, Altissimi, Regis, Domini, qui cuncta creavit Amen.

Expansion

Vinculum & Allocutio

Ego NN ligo et vinculo te Spiritus N per hunc horam hoc loco *dia tou theou* Patrem & Filium, & Spiritum Sanctum et per novem ordines Angelorum, salvete ergo Spiritus quia vos vocavi per illum cui omne genu flectitur, Coelestium, Terrestrium, et Infernorum, cuius in manu omnia regna Regnum sunt, nec est qui suae contrarius esse possit Majestati, quatenus nunc constringo vos ut hic ante Circulum visibiles et affabiles permaneatis, tamdiu tamque constantes, nec sine permissione et licentia recidatis, donec meam sine fallacia aliqua et veridice perficiatis voluntatem, [p. 16] per Potentiæ illius virtutem qui Mare posuit Terminum suum, quem praeterire non potest, et lege illius Potentiae non pertransit fines suos, Dei, Altissimi, Regis, Domini, qui cuncta creavit, Amen.[2]

---

[1] *Genesis* 4:1.

[2] Cf. *Heptameron*: Ego N. N. ligo et vinculo te spiritus N per hunc horam hoc loco dei *tou theou* Patrem & Filium & Spiritum Sanctum et per Novem ordines Angelorum, sabete ergo quia vos vocavi per illum cui omne genu flectitur, coelestium, terrestrium et infernorum: cuius in manu omnia regna regum sunt, nec est qui suæ contrarius esse possit majestati. Quatenus nunc constringo vos, ut hic ante circulum, visibiles et affabiles permaneatis, tamdiu tamque constantes, nec sine permissione et licentia recedatis, donec meam sine fallacia aliqua et veredicem perficiatis voluntatem, per potentiæ illius virtutem, qui mari posuit terminum suum, quem præterire non potest, et lege illius potentiæ non pertransit fines suos, Dei altissimi, regis, domini, qui cuncta creavit, Amen.

Translation

Binding & Address

I [Name] tie and bind you Spirit [Name] at this hour to here reside by the Lord God, Father & Son & Holy Spirit, and by the nine orders of Angels. Welcome therefore Spirit, for I have called you by him to whom every knee bends, in heaven, on earth and in the hells, in whose hand are all the kingdoms of Kings, nor is there anyone who can stand against his Majesty, whereby I constrain you now that you remain visible and affable before this Circle, as long and as constantly [as I wish], nor without permission and license may you depart, until you have granted my wish truly and without any deception, [p.16] by virtue of the power of him who set the sea its bounds, which it cannot transgress, nor cross its limits by the law of his power, of God, the most high, the King, the Lord who created all things, Amen.

Text

Ter Repete

Fuga Daemonum

Audi Tu ad verba mea mihi obediens, et voluntatem meam explere consuete Ω NN. abi jam rursus in locum tuum ubi fuisti antequam Te advocavi huc donec Ego Volente Deo Te iterum vocavero, sisq[uam] semper paratus venire vocatus p[er] nomi[ne] vivi & veri, & Invincibilis Dei Trementissimi atq[ue] Fortissimi, [p. 17] Ego vero ex Lege illius Majestatis Thesaurum in Citatione praemissa postulatum abs te accipio et auffero; Abi nunc Placatissime in locum tuum sine rumore, Tumultu et sine laesione nostrum et circuli aliorumq[ue] hominum, in Nomine Patris + et Filii + & Spiritus Sancti + Amen.

IHS

Expansion

Ter Repete

Fuga Daemonum

Audi Tu ad verba mea mihi obediens, et voluntatem meam explere consuete Spiritus NN. abi jam rursus in locum tuum ubi fuisti antequam Te advocavi huc donec Ego Volente Deo Te iterum vocavero, sisquam semper paratus venire vocatus per nomine vivi & veri, & Invincibilis Dei Trementissimi atque Fortissimi, [p. 17] Ego vero ex Lege illius Majestatis Thesaurum in Citatione praemissa postulatum abs te accipio et auffero; Abi nunc Placatissime in locum tuum sine rumore, Tumultu et sine laesione nostrum et circuli aliorumque hominum, in Nomine Patris + et Filii + & Spiritus Sancti + Amen.

I H S

Translation

Thrice Repeat

Banishment of the Demons [1]

Hear my words, obey me, and be accustomed to fulfil my wish Spirit [Name] go now back again to your place where you were before I called you here, until I, God Willing, again call you, and be always ready to come [when] called by the name of the Living and True and Invincible God, most dreadful and strong, and I may from the law of his Majesty receive and take away from you the treasure[2] asked for in the aforesaid summoning; go now most peacefully to your place without murmur, tumult and without injury to us and the circle or to other men, in the Name of the Father + and the Son + and Holy Spirit +, Amen.

Jesus [3]

---

[1] The License to Depart. Literally "demons flee."

[2] The mention of treasure here is reminiscent of the Spanish Cyprianus which concentrated on the finding of treasure by magic in the province of Galicia.

[3] In the Christianity of mediaeval Western Europe, the most common initials for Jesus Christ were 'IHS' from the first three letters of the Greek name of Jesus, ΙΗΣ. Here the Greek letter *eta* is transliterated as the letter 'H' in the Latin-speaking West. 'IHS' is sometimes interpreted as meaning *Iesus Hominum Salvator* ('Jesus, Savior of men') or connected with *In Hoc Signo*. The historian Eusebius states that the Emperor Constantine I was marching with his army, when he looked up to the sun and saw a cross of light above it, and with it the Greek words "εν τούτω νίκα" ("by this, be victorious!", often rendered in Latin as *In hoc signo vinces*). This acronym has been used in Latin since the seventh century.

Text

[p. 18]

Tunc Scribito.

S.A. I I R I V I D S T N
[con]tra omne M C & A.

Dimissio scribatur

VᵖXИUUmUUmVVɔX. ЧX itt ω̑

VᵖXδИꟻϿ⊙ȗVᵖЧNω̑VVɔИ

ЧV≠XΛꟻ a quoquam, VXV

ԿmЧ+ӿ╤ϴTUX.

+ ♈ + Meotorile + + Lei + Pelei +
Jonar + Jonar + Psui +
Ofstam +

Expansion

Tunc Scribito.

S.A. I I R I V I D S T N
contra omne M C & A.

Dimissio scribatur

CORAPPAPPAE. IN itt ω̑

COδRꟻ[Moon?] [Sun]ȗCINω̑AR

IVPhXNꟻ a quoquam, BXC

ԿPPI+M╤ϴTAX.

+ ♈ + Meotorile + + Lei + Pelei +
Jonar + Jonar + Psui +
Ofstam +

Translation

Then Write.[1]

S.A. I I R I V I D S T N
Against all M C & A.

This Dismissal is written

CORAPPAPPAE. IN itt ῶ

COδRℲ[Moon?] [Sun] ῦLCINῶAR

IVPhXNℲ anywhere, BXC

ҺPPIᵻMϘϑTAX.

+ ♈ + Meotorile + + Lei + Pelei +
Jonar + Jonar + Psui +
Ofstam +

[1] This is a written dismissal, and should probably be written in the original characters, rather than transliterated.

Appendix I - Table of Magical Scripts [1]

Paths on Tree of Life.		*Reference Hebrew Alphabet.*	L47. Celestial Characters.	L48. Crossing the River.	L49. Malachim Script.	L50. Alphabet of the Magi.
	1					
	2					
	3					
	4					
	5					
	6					
	7					
	8					
	9					
	10					
A	11	Aleph				
☿	12	Beth				
☾	13	Gimel				
♀	14	Daleth				
♈	15	He				
♉	16	Vav				
♊	17	Zayin				
♋	18	Cheth				
♌	19	Teth				
♍	20	Yod				
♃	21	Kaph				
♎	22	Lamed				
W	23	Mem				
♏	24	Nun				
♐	25	Samekh				
♑	26	Ayin				
♂	27	Peh				
♒	28	Tzaddi				
♓	29	Qoph				
☼	30	Resh				
F	31	Shin				
♄	32	Tau				

[1] From Stephen Skinner, *Complete Magician's Table,* Golden Hoard Press, London, 2006.

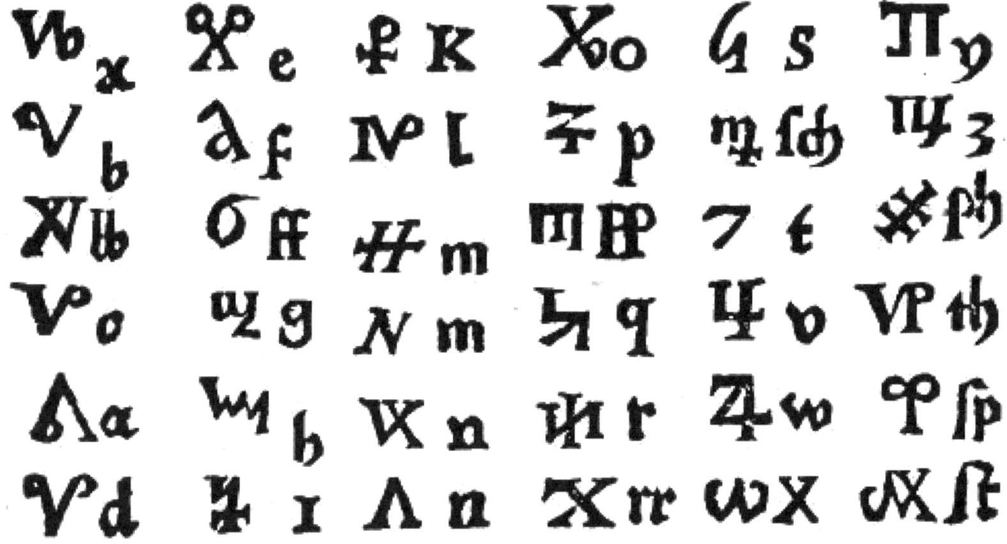

The alphabet of Cyprian from Harley MS 3420 the *Magical Calendar* 1614.[1] This is used in the encoding of the last page of the *Clavis Inferni.*

DE POLYGRAPHIE. 186

a	e	k	o	s	y
b	f	l	p	sch	z
bb	ff	m	pp	t	ph
c	g	m	q	u	th
cc	h	n	r	&	ſp
d	i	n	rr	x	ſt

The alphabet of Cicero and Cyprian from Trithemius's *Polygraphia,* 1561.

[1] Note that as well as a full alphabet there are also single characters for the combinations bb, cc, ff, pp, rr, and more common ligatures such as sch, ph, th, sp, and st. In addition there are two values for both 'm' and 'n', a total of 36 characters.

Appendix III – Other Grimoire Citations of St Cyprian

The Angelical Citation of St Cyprian [1]

I call - cause - cite - and exorcise thee: O Almaziel Ariel Anathamia Ezebul Abiul Ezea Ahesin and Calizabin – by the most Holy Angels of God by all the dominations thrones powers and angelical principalities by all the beatitudes and ineffable delights of Heaven.

By the Angel which announced to the Shepherd the Incarnation and nativity of the Saviour - by the four and twenty elders who cry incessantly before the Divine throne. Holy Holy Holy is the Lord our God and by the Holy intercourse of the Angels who have the Knowledge of Jesus, by the Cherubim and by the Seraphim and by all the archangels - by the infinity and omnipotency of God and by the creation of the world - that thou helpest me in this my need even as thou didst assist Lot and Abraham who were your hosts - as also Jacob and Moses, Joshua and Samson and many others whom you have deigned to visit - come o ye angelic ones in beautiful form, full of dignity and brightness - and do all that which I have requested thee - in the name of the Triune Jehovah whose praises all spirits incessantly sing, giving honour to the all Powerful who is thy Lord as he is mine.

Amen

Dimissio Cypriani [2]

Conjuro nunc te, o Spiritus humane! per omnipotentissimi Dei Patris sapientiam atque justitiam: per omnipotentissimi Dei Filii immensam erga miseros nos homines misericordiam et caritatem; per omnipotentissimi Spiritus Sancti infinitam sapientiam atque inscrutabilem elementiam per sanctum Michaëlem, archangelum omnemque coeli militiam, ut pacifice pro nunc et quiete absque corruscationibus, meticuloso ac tremendo strepitu et tumultu sine pluviis, vel tonitruis, et uno verbo: sine periculo, sive animae, sive corporis noxa et damno, vel laesione discedas, locumque hunc nunquam prius, nisi citatus, accedas. Trinunius Dei pax descendat jam super nos et custodiat nos! Illuminet Dominus vultum suum super nos et miseriatur nostri! Convertat Dominus vultum suum ad nos et dat nobis pacem! Amen!

---

[1] From the *Libellus Magicus* ('The Little Book of Magic'), Paris, 1508 [sic]. A. E. Waite's copy of a manuscript translation made in 1875 by Herbert Irwin, folio 24.

[2] From the *Verus Jesuitarum Libellus* ('The True Little Book of the Jesuits') from Volume 2 of Johann Scheible's *Das Kloster*.

Appendix IV – The Seven Candlesticks of Revelation by Albrecht Dürer

Figure 12: A well-known engraving entitled 'St. John beholding the seven candlesticks' by Albrecht Dürer shows the traditional symbolic attributes of the Holy Spirit. Compare with Figure 6.

Bibliography

Manuscript Source

Wellcome MS 2000

Printed Books

Abano, Peter de, *Heptameron or Magical Elements*. See Agrippa *Fourth Book of Occult Philosophy*.

Abraham of Worms, *The Book of Abramelin*, Ibis, Lake Worth, 2006. [Edited by Georg Dehn, translated by Steven Guth].

Agrippa, H. C. *Three Books of Occult Philosophy*. Translated by James Freake [Dr John French]. Edited by Donald Tyson. Llewellyn, St Paul, 1993.

Agrippa, H. C. *Fourth Book of Occult Philosophy*.
First facsimile edition Askin Publishers, London, 1978. It includes:
Of Occult Philosophy, or Magical Ceremonies by Agrippa;
Heptameron or Magical Elements by Peter de Abano;
Isagoge: On the Nature of Such Spirits by Georg Villinganus;
Arbatel of Magick: *Of the Magick of the Ancients* by Agrippa;
Of Geomancy by Agrippa;
Of Astronomical Geomancy by Gerard Cremonensis.
A modernised edition by Stephen Skinner, Ibis Press, Berwick, 2005.

Ankarloo, Bengt, & Clark, Stuart, *Witchcraft and Magic in Europe, Volume 3: The Middle Ages*, University of Pennsylvania Press, Pennsylvania, 2002.

Butler, Elizabeth, *Ritual Magic,* CUP, Cambridge, 1949.

Charbonneau-Lassay, Louis, *The Bestiary of Christ*, Arkana, London, 1991.

Couliano, Ioan P, *Eros and Magic in the Renaissance,* University of Chicago Press, Chicago, 1987.

Davies, Owen, *Grimoires: a History of Magic Books,* OUP, Oxford, 2009.

De Claremont, Lewis, *The Ancient's Book of Magic*, Oracle, 1936.

Elior, Rachel, *The Three Temples: On the Emergence of Jewish Mysticism*, Littman Library of Jewish Civilization, Oregon, 2005.

Fanger, Claire [ed], *Conjuring Spirits: Texts and Traditions of Medieval Ritual Magic,* Pennsylvania State UP & Sutton Publishing, 1998.

Faust, Doktor Johannes, *Faust's Magia Naturalis et Innaturalis, oder Dreifacher Höllen-zwang, letztes Testament und Siegelkunst. Nach einer kostbar ausgestatteten Handschrift in der Herzogl. Bibliothek zu Koburg vollständig und wortgetreu herausgeben in fünf Abtheilungen mit einer Menge illuminirter Abbildungen auf 146 Tafeln,* Verlage von J Scheible, Stuttgart, 1848 reprinted Verlag Richard Schikowski, Berlin, 1995.

Gettings, Fred, *Dictionary of Occult, Hermetic and Alchemical Sigils,* Routledge, London, 1981.

Gruenwald, Ithamar, *Apocalyptic and Merkavah Mysticism*, Brill, Leiden, 1980.

Horst, J. C., *Zauberbibliothek,* 6 volumes, Mainz, 1821-26.

Jackson, Howard M., 'A Contribution toward an Edition of the *Confession* of Cyprian of Antioch: the *Secreta Cypriani*', in *Muséon* 1001, 1988, pages 33-41.

James, Geoffrey, *Angel Magic: the Ancient Art of Summoning and Communicating with Angelic Beings,* Llewellyn, St. Paul, 1997.

Kieckhefer, Richard, *Forbidden Rites: A Necromancer's Manual of the Fifteenth Century,* Sutton, Stroud, 1997.

Kuntz, Darcy [edited], *Ars Notoria: the Magical Art of Solomon…Englished by Robert Turner,* Holmes, Sequim, 2006. [First English edition 1656].

Levi, Eliphas, *The History of Magic,* Rider, London, 1974, page 168.

Lieberman, Saul, 'Metatron, the Meaning of His Name and His Functions' in Ithamar Gruenwald, *Apocalyptic and Merkavah Mysticism*, Leiden, Brill, 1980.

Leitch, Aaron, *Secrets of the Magical Grimoires*, Llewellyn, Woodbury, 2005.

Lisiewski, Joseph C, *Ceremonial Magic & The Power of Evocation*, New Falcon, Tempe, Arizona, 2004.

MacDonald, Michael Albion, *De Nigromancia [attributed to] Roger Bacon*, Heptangle Books, New Jersey, 1987.

Mathers, S L MacGregor, (trans.) *The Key of Solomon the King (Clavicula Salomonis),* Redway 1889 and Kegan Paul, London, 1909.

Meyer, Marvin & Smith, Richard, *Ancient Christian Magic: Coptic Texts of Ritual Power,* Princeton University Press, Princeton, New Jersey, 1999, pages 153-58.

Odeberg, Hugo, *3 Enoch or The Hebrew Book of Enoch*, Cambridge University Press, Cambridge, 1928.

Orlov, Andrei A, *The Enoch-Metatron Tradition*, Mohr-Siebeck, Tuebingen, 2005.

Peterson, Joseph, http://www.esotericarchives.com.

Peterson, Joseph, *Lesser Key of Solomon,* Weiser, York Beach, 2001.

Peterson, Joseph, *Sixth and Seventh Book of Moses,* Ibis, Berwick, 2008.

Pingree, David, (editor) *Picatrix: The Latin Version of the Ghayat al-Hakim*, Warburg Institute, London, 1986.

Quispel, G., 'An Unknown Fragment of the Acts of Andrew' in *Gnostic Studies II*, Nederlands Historisch-Archaeologisch Instituut, Istanbul, 1975, pages 271-87.

Radermacher, L, *Griechische Quellen zur Faustsage*, Vienna, 1927.

Reitzenstein, R, 'Cyprian der Magier', in *NGWG, PH*, 1917, pages 38-79.

Sabattini, P, 'S. Cipriano nella Tradizione Agiografica', in *RSC*, 21, 1973, pages 181-204.

Scheible, Johann, *Das Kloster*, Stuttgart and Leipzig, 12 volumes, 1845-1849.

Scholem, Gershom, *Major Trends in Jewish Mysticism*, Schocken, New York, 1995.

Scot, Reginald, *Discoverie of Witchcraft*, Elliot Stock, London, 1886, reprinted from 1665 edition. [limited edition of 250 copies], Book xv, Chapter i-iv, pages 376-329 *et seq*.

Shah, Sayed Idries, *The Secret Lore of Magic*, Muller, London, 1957.

Skinner, Stephen, *Complete Magician's Tables*, Golden Hoard Press, London & Singapore, 2006; second edition Llewellyn, Woodbury, 2007.

Skinner, Stephen & Rankine, David, *The Practical Angel Magic of Dr. John Dee's Enochian Tables*, Volume 1 Sourceworks of Ceremonial Magic, Golden Hoard Press, London, 2004.

Skinner, Stephen & Rankine, David, *Keys to the Gateway of Magic*, Volume 2 Sourceworks of Ceremonial Magic, Golden Hoard Press, London, 2005.

Skinner, Stephen & Rankine, David, *The Goetia of Dr Rudd*, Volume 3 Sourceworks of Ceremonial Magic, Golden Hoard Press, London, 2007.

Skinner, Stephen & Rankine, David, *The Veritable Key of Solomon*, Volume 4 Sourceworks of Ceremonial Magic, Golden Hoard Press, London, 2008 and Llewellyn, 2008.

Thompson, R. Campbell, *Semitic Magic*, Samuel Weiser Inc, Maine, 2000.

Tritheme, J, *Polygraphie*, 1561. [Trithemius's *Polygraphia*]

Waite, A E, *The Book of Black Magic and of Pacts*, Privately Printed, Edinburgh, 1898, republished by Samuel Weiser, York Beach, 1972.

Waite, A. E., *The Secret Tradition in Goetia*, Rider, London, 1911.

Waite, A. E., *The Book of Ceremonial Magic*, University Books, New York, 1961.

Scandinavian Cyprianus

Amundsen, Arne, *Svartebøken fra Borge,* Sarpsborg, 1987.

Bang, Anton, 'Svartebøgen' in *Kirkehistoriske Smaastykker Kristiania,* Cammermeyer, 1890, pages 336-48.

Bang, Anton, *Norske Hexe-Formularer og Magiske Opskrifte,* Kristiana, 1901-1902.

Bo, Olav, 'Trollformler' in *Kulturhistorisk Leksikon for Nordisk Middelalder,* 2nd edition, 24 vols, Rosenkilde og Bagger, Copenhagen, 1982, Volume 18, pages 674-8.

Cyprianus, *Oldtidens Sortebog fra Aaret 1400,* [John Anderson], Chicago, 1892.

Espeland, Velle, *Svartbøka,* Oslo Universitetsforlaget, Oslo, 1974.

Feilberg, H. F., 'Cyprianus' in *Aarbog for Dansk Kulturhistorie,* 1897, pages 97-124.

Garstein, Oscar,*Vinjeboka: Den eldste Svartebøka fra norsk middelalder,* Solum Forlag, Oslo, 1993.

Grambo, Ronald, *Norske Trylleformler,* Universitetsforlager, Oslo, 1979.

Hansen, H. P., *Kloge Folk,* Copenhagen, 1960.

Herr, Karl, *Hex and Spellwork: The Magical Practices of the Pennsylvania Dutch,* RedWheel Weiser, York Beach, 2002.

Hodnebo, Finn, 'Trolldomsboker' in *Kulturhistorisk Leksikon for Nordisk Middelalder,* 2nd edition, 24 vols, Rosenkilde og Bagger, Copenhagen, 1982, Volume 18, pages 670-4.

Hohman, John George, *Pow-Wows; The Long Lost Friend, a collection of Mysterious & Invaluable Arts and Remedies,* USA, 1820 reprinted 1856.

Kokborg, Henrik, *En Lille Udtog af Syprianus* ['A Little Portion of Syprianus'], Denmark, c. 1890.

McBryde, John M. Jr., 'Some Medieval Charms' in *Sewanee Review,* 1917, Vol 25 (July), pages 292-304.

Munthe, Wilhelm, 'Svartebøka' in *Festkrift til Hjalmar Pettersen,* Steenske Forlag, Oslo, 1926, pages 86-93.

Naess, Hans Eyvind, *Trolldomsprosessene i Norge pa 1500-1600 tallet,* Universitetsforlaget, Oslo, 1982.

Nyerup, Rasmus, *Almindelig Morskabslosning i Danmark og Norge igjennem Aarhundreder,* Andreas Seidelins Forlag, Kobenhavn, 1816.

Osland, Birgir, *A Long Pull from Stavanger: The Reminiscences of a Norwegian Immigrant,* Norwegian American Historical Association, Northfield, 1945.

Pio, Iorn, ed, *Cyprianus,* Immanual Ree's Forlag, Kobenhavn, 1870.

Reichborn-Kjennerud, *Var gamle Trolldomsmedisin*, 5, Dybwad, Oslo, 1927-47.

Rosenlund, Sören ['Junior Philopatreias'], *Sybrianus P. P. P.*, Denmark, 1771.

Rustad, Mary, *The Black Books of Elverum*, Galde, Lakeville, Minnesota, 2006.

Saebo, Asbjorn, 'Svartebøka' in *Romsdal Sogelag Aarsskrift,* Romsdal Historielag, Molde, 1966.

Skatvedt, Thormod, *Sigdal og Eggedal V: Historisk beretning utarbeidet efter foranstaltning av, Sigdals herredsstyre*, edited Andreas Morch, Sigdal og Eggedal Historielag, Amot, 1914.

Stokker, Kathleen, 'Migratory Legend 3005'; `The Would-Be Ghost'; 'Why Be he a Ghost?'; 'Lutheran Views of Confession and Salvation' in *Legends of the Black Book Minister,* Yearbook of Scandinavian Folklore, Arv, 1991, Volume 47, pages 143-52.

Stokker, Kathleen, 'Between Sin and Salvation: The Human Condition in Legends of the Black Book Minister', in *Scandinavian Studies,* 1995, Volume 67.1, 1995, pages 91-108.

Stokker, Kathleen, 'Secrets of the Black Book: Folk Medicine in Norwegian-America' in *The Norseman*, November 1995.

Stokker, Kathleen, 'To Catch a Thief: Binding and Loosing and the Black Book Minister' in *Scandinavian Studies*, 1989, 61.4, pages 353-74.

Stokker, Kathleen, *Keeping Christmas: Yuletide Traditions in Norway and the New Land*, Minnesota Historical Society, St Paul, 2000.

Stokker, Kathleen, 'Narratives of Magic and Healing: *Oldtidens Sortebog* in Norway and the New Land' in *Scandinavian Studies*, 2001.

Stokker, Kathleen, 'The Black Book in the New Land: Norwegian American Perceptions of Illness and Healing,' paper delivered at the Vandringer Conference at the Minnesota Historical Society, St. Paul, 2000.

Iberian Cyprianus

Ciprien Mago ante Conversionem, Salamanca, 1460 [*sic*].

Libro de San Cipriano (The Book of St Ciprian).

O Antigo Livro de São Cipriano (The Ancient Book of St Ciprian).

O Verdadeiro e Último Livro de São Cipriano (The True and Last Book of Saint Ciprian), São Paulo, 1916.

The Authentic Book of St. Cyprian.

The Great and True Book of St. Cyprian.

The Only Complete Book of St. Cyprian.

Vicente, Félix Francisco, 'El Libro de San Cipriano (I and II)' in *Hibris,* Volume 27-28, 2005.

Missler, Peter , 'Las Hondas Raices del Ciprianillo' second part 'los grimorios' in *Culturas Populares, Revista Electronica 3,* September-December 2006.

Varela, Bernardo, *Brujos y Astrologos de la Inquisicion de Galicia y el famoso libro de San Cipriano,* Madrid, 1885 reprinted 1973, pages 259-288.

INDEX